There is a great crisis in our generation. Marriages and families are in desperate need. This is the first generation in which children are influenced more outside their home than in it. We believe this book will help bring solutions and strength to marriages and homes in this generation!

This is a much-needed book in the body of Christ. We are happy that Antonio and Christelle have written *House on Fire: Revival Begins in the Home.*

MIKE AND DIANE BICKLE
Founders, International House of Prayer
Kansas City, Missouri

House on Fire: Revival Begins in the Home by Antonio and Christelle Baldovinos is filled with powerful truth that conveys the magnificence of God. As you immerse yourself in the written words, hope begins to rise and faith is activated, causing a "yes, Lord" to flow from your heart. Suddenly, your beliefs are aligned with God's, and that which once seemed impossible is now possible. I highly recommend this life-changing book!

DR. CHÉ AHN
HRock Church
Pasadena, California

One of the best ways that you can gauge your love for Jesus is to look at the way you love your spouse and your children. My wife, Lindsey, and I have had the honor of seeing this truth lived out in the lives of our great friends, Antonio and Christelle Baldovinos.

Their new book, *House on Fire*, is a much-needed resource that sheds light on the question that the apostle Paul asks Timothy, "If a man cannot manage his own household, how can he take care of God's church?" I encourage you to light your marriage and family candle on the flame of this book!

Rick Pino

Heart of David Worship and Missions Center

Austin, Texas

The family is the most basic institution of all societies. In the western world, it is under a savage attack—greater than most places of the world. Christelle and Antonio are writing a book that will challenge the status quo and the erosion of the family in nations that have been considered Christian for more than 500 years.

As the authors have a solid marriage and a fruitful ministry, they write from a strong foundation, both biblical and personal, to start a major conversation among Christians by making radical suggestions to stir up not only the thinking, but a spirit and hunger for God's answer and for a movement of transformation of the family and marriage.

May God bless you in your discoveries with Him, and may this book be an inspiration for your life and, through you, the lives of others.

Loren Cunningham

Founder, Youth With A Mission

HOUSE on FIRE

REVIVAL BEGINS IN THE HOME

ANTONIO & CHRISTELLE BALDOVINOS

DESTINY IMAGE® PUBLISHERS, INC.

P.O. Box 310, Shippensburg, PA 17257-0310

"Promoting Inspired Lives."

This book and all other Destiny Image and Destiny Image Fiction books are available at Christian bookstores and distributors worldwide.

Cover design by Christian Rafetto

For more information on foreign distributors, call 717-532-3040.

Reach us on the Internet: www.destinyimage.com.

ISBN 13 TP: 978-0-7684-0679-5

ISBN 13 eBook: 978-0-7684-0680-1

For Worldwide Distribution, Printed in the U.S.A.

1 2 3 4 5 6 7 8 / 19 18 17 16 15

DEDICATION

We dedicate this book to our parents—Mark and Karen Anderson and Carlos and Sandra Baldovinos. We are standing on your shoulders today. We are so thankful for you—the battles you fought and the price you paid for us to have the blessings that we have. Your legacy lives on, and the inheritance you have given us will be passed on to the next generations!

ACKNOWLEDGMENTS

God never intended for anyone to do anything of significance alone. The message of this book was done with the help of many friends. We want to thank Joyce Stigter, Kirsten Mark, Ian Byrd, Randi Short, and Jeff and Mary Printz. Your countless hours proofing and editing are a lot of work. We are indebted to you and are very grateful. Thank you for believing in us and the message of this book!

CONTENTS

Foreword   *by Bob and Audrey Meisner* 13

Introduction   Revival Begins in the Home 17

Chapter 1   Countercultural................................. 21

Chapter 2   Establishing Foundations........................ 45

Chapter 3   The Fight for Marriage.......................... 73

Chapter 4   Pruning that Leads to Intimacy.................. 99

Chapter 5   The Glory of Fathers........................... 117

Chapter 6   Embracing Motherhood........................... 145

Chapter 7   Aiming Your Arrows 165

Chapter 8   Dating God's Way............................... 181

Chapter 9   A Prophetic Home 201

Chapter 10   A Thousand Generations......................... 219

                Endnotes....................................... 237

FOREWORD

R*evive our hearts, oh Lord, set them ablaze with Your presence!"* This is the cry we have repeatedly heard within the marriages and families concerned for their own homes, neighborhoods, and communities. Nothing thrills our hearts more than the prospect of God's glory being manifested to our world through the lives of His people.

The resounding cry and heart of this message is not so much against the evils of a lost world as it is to the heart of the family, which is at the heart of the church. There is a growing desperation, not from a sense of lack, but rather for a singleness of heart, clarity of vision, and purpose for our homes and families.

We believe it's time to sound an alarm! Set your home ablaze with the power and fire of the Holy Spirit. Joel 2:1 says, *"Blow the trumpet in Zion, and sound an alarm in My holy mountain! ...For the day of the Lord is coming."* There is a certain sound that initiates movement and awareness. In times past, the trumpet would sound to let the people know that it was time to assemble for war; now, it signals that it is time to appropriate to our lives our inheritance found in the finished work of Jesus.

Some listen to the alerts of worry, while others are tuned out and complacent in their current cultural and technological surroundings. The problem is that neither are paying attention to the warning system within them, which is activated by the Holy Spirit. When we hear the alarm, we can respond properly and, as a result, realize victory at the end of any situation. We may not have all the answers, but we will have a peace that passes our understanding. What truly matters in a world like ours is having and keeping this peace, which determines how we will advance in our journey.

God has given us the power of the Holy Spirit to win every battle that carries a threat against our home and family. However, if we are anxiously walking in the fear of the future and are distracted by all of the "stressors" in the world around us, we may possibly miss the warning signs of our heart. We need knowledge, understanding, and wisdom that come from the mouth of God. When our heart is in tune to the voice of the Lord, we will be immovable—we will see the glory of the Lord ablaze in our homes.

We will never forget the first time Antonio and Christelle walked into our TV studio to record programs. As we discussed options for teaching topics, they both lit up as they began to tell us the story about how *everything* changed when the Holy Spirit caught fire in their home. That kind of passion, beauty, and supernatural expression is as contagious as a fire. It felt like they were double-dog daring us to connect with the Holy Spirit as they intrigued us with their new disciplines and discoveries that set their home apart as a shining example of light. The response was tremendous as people heard hope for their families and a fresh word from God's heart.

You will experience the power of God in your life when your heart catches fire with the Holy Spirit. His power enables you to be His witness throughout the world, accomplishing a mission and adventure you cannot carry out in your own strength. Jesus promised the Holy Spirit to His disciples just prior to His ascension to Heaven, emphasizing the Spirit's importance in their lives, homes, and ministry.

As you embark on this adventure of experiencing a "house on fire," you may be thinking, "Yes, God can involve Himself in families, but I am completely without resources. My family is broken." If that is you, then you need to know that the less you can do, the more God's power can accomplish in and through you. Paul learned this secret when God told him, *"Power is made perfect in weakness"* (2 Cor. 12:9 NIV). The weaker you are, the better God's power can perform. Even when you are down, you are never out, despite what the world may say! God's infinite power can accomplish the seemingly impossible in His plan, in His way, in His time, and in His extraordinary, supernatural power.

Jesus loves to share secrets with the childlike ones, the ones who depend on Him. Antonio and Christelle have tapped into secrets given to them from Father God's heart. As your family catches fire for Jesus and the fire spreads everywhere, it will ignite other hearts and draw them to know, love, and live for the Lord. This book will empower you to experience God's plan, person, presence, power, and purpose for your family. The presence of the Lord is going to burn on fire for Jesus Christ in your hearts, and your family will never be the same.

Within the pages of this book you will be given an opportunity to activate your faith and be invited to walk in restoration and recovery for your home. You will not only avoid the terror of the night and the danger of the day, but your home will experience the true comfort of the Holy Spirit that will set you ablaze, making you a contagious flame of hope to families around the world.

Sound the alarm; your home is about to catch fire with the love of God, and nothing will stand in the way of His dream for your family.

Congratulations to Antonio and Christelle for running with the torch to fight for families! We are honored to be part of your story and thankful to call you our close friends.

Bob and Audrey Meisner

Best-selling authors, *Marriage Under Cover*

Television Hosts, mynewday.tv

REVIVAL BEGINS IN THE HOME

Let your families be trained in the fear of God and
be yourselves "holiness unto the Lord"; so shall
you stand like a rock amid the surging waves of
error and ungodliness which rage around us.
—Charles Spurgeon*

There is an unholy momentum building as attacks are mounting against marriages, parenting, and the identity of our children today. There is an all-out war aimed at removing all moral boundaries within our culture, including the sanctity of life, marriage, and sexuality. The greatest revival and the greatest disaster that the world has ever known are just ahead of us. For the human race, our best days and our worst days are quickly approaching.

Surrounded by crisis and the abolishing of biblical truth, God desires to raise up homes as the place to nurture, love, and train the next generation with power. The times we are living in necessitate revival, and revival begins in the home.

DEFINING HISTORY

Human history has been defined by the responses of people amidst crises. It is full of people whose decisions under pressure intervened and shaped history. May 19, 2008 was a history-defining time for our family. After being in full-time ministry for over a decade, we were in a state of crisis. Our home was compromised.

Engrossed in secular entertainment of all kinds, the indulgence of vain appetites had led us into a trap. We were faced with the repercussions of what we had sown for too long. I (Antonio) was injecting steroids and watching pornography. I (Christelle) was going through all the "motions" of Christianity yet was full of self-righteousness and apathy. Our children knew more about the latest movie than about the person and work of Jesus.

After years of ministry, our lives had become a mere shadow of Christian living. What had once been zeal for God had now become only form, with a heart that was distant from God at best. We had biblical "beliefs," but rarely did our lives behind closed doors reflect them. God wanted so much more for us, and deep down so did we. But how do we get more? We had to face the condition of our hearts and home and respond to God's light and grace.

IMAGINE AND DREAM

Two months after radically shifting our lives and marriage, God led us to imagine and dream once again. So we took out our journal and we began to write. Although seemingly impossible at the time, we made a list of dreams, and we were shocked to watch the very things we wrote on that list be fulfilled within months. We had now embarked on a new frontier of hope. What we imagined came true.

The power of God was released upon our cold hearts and our once side-by-side marriage. Miraculously, God turned us toward each other to have a face-to-face relationship with each other, but also with Him. We are now living those dreams, and, as a result, our children have flourished. What once seemed beyond our grasp has now become our reality.

COMFORT VERSUS PEACE

In Second Kings 20, we read the sobering story of King Hezekiah, who had walked with God. Upon contracting a severe illness and being faced with death, he cried out to God. God heard him and extended his life by 15 years. Shortly after being healed, Hezekiah sinned by showing the wealth and accolades of his kingdom to the Babylonian king and arrogantly took credit for it all. God invoked His verdict through the prophet Isaiah by saying, *"And they shall take away some of your sons who will descend from you, whom you will beget; and they shall be eunuchs in the palace of the king of Babylon"* (2 Kings 20:18).

Hezekiah's response to this was outrageous. He said, *"At least there will peace and security during my lifetime"* (2 Kings 20:19 NLT). When Hezekiah was threatened with his own personal distress and death, he desperately cried out to God. But when confronted with the outcome of future generations, his apathy and selfishness was horribly devastating.

The destiny of humankind is before you and me. The story of our families is not written by chance, but by choice and action. We must fight for something bigger than ourselves. We too must echo the words of President Harry S. Truman, which were so simply yet profoundly stated: "Our goal must be—not peace in our time—but peace for all time."[1]

JOIN US

This book you now hold in your hands was birthed out of God's mercy and transforming power. The biblical truths it contains revived our lives and our home, as well as the lives of the many we have been privileged to share it with. Our hope and prayer is that this book will awaken within you a desire to be an agent who brings revival to your home and the generations after you.

A fire needs a spark. Hence, we are impelled to write. We hope the message of this book fans a flame for your home to be a *House on Fire*.

Passionate for revival in the home,
Antonio and Christelle

Chapter 1

COUNTERCULTURAL

Our times demand it. Our history compels it.
Our future requires it. And God is watching.
—Rod Parsley, *Silent No More**

Have you ever heard the saying, "Beware of Greeks bearing gifts" or the myth of the Trojan horse? Perhaps you've heard of the story once told of two great kingdoms—Greece and Troy. These two adversaries fought each other for almost ten years. The war included treachery, an oath to protect a marriage, a bribe of love, and an enormous impenetrable wall.

The resilience Troy displayed was legendary. Thousands of ships gathered and as many Greeks died trying to penetrate the city's massive wall. Despite losing virtually all its greatest champions, Troy still would not fall. The city's walls were seemingly impassable.

After many years of battle, legend states the Greeks came up with an ingenious yet risky plan to get inside the city's great walls. They proceeded to construct an enormous wooden horse that would be given to the city of Troy as a victory gift. Little did the city residents know a band of Greek warriors was hiding inside the horse and waiting to prey upon their pride. A small army of the boldest warriors presented this gift to Troy and then appeared to set sail for a return trip to Greece. They only traveled, however, to the far side of the city's shore.

When the Trojans found the horse (which had a special inscription dedicating it to the Greek goddess Athena), some wanted to burn it or push it off a cliff. Others argued, however, that if they brought it inside the city's walls it would bring them luck. They chose to bring it in. Following the drunken celebration of their victory, the Trojans collapsed into bed. While they were sleeping, the Greek warriors inside the horse left their hiding place, opened the city gates, and seized Troy in a single bloody night.

Why do we start this first chapter with a mythical story about two kingdoms and an impenetrable wall? Because we believe there's been a Greek horse placed inside our homes. If we could discern the danger, it would never garner such a prominent place—even though it seems harmless and insignificant. In many ways, what's entered has crept in unnoticed, and our apathy to the dangers of seemingly harmless things has left us unprepared and asleep. We celebrate in a drunken stupor, allowing a gigantic horse to overtake us.

Our hope is that a great wake-up call goes out to every home and is heard before it's too late. If there are hidden and dangerous devices of the enemy in your life, your marriage, or your home, then we hope this book—our story and the principles we've learned—will help you begin a journey toward wholeness and a new sense of God's grace and wisdom.

OUR HOME

On May 19, 2008, God spoke to me (Christelle) and said, "A storm is coming!" At the time I rarely heard from God, but I knew the words echoing within were from Him.

That night, as I (Antonio) walked through our door, I knew something was different—things were never going to be the same again. The confusion etched across Christelle's face as she sat crying on our bed filled me with shock. "What is going on?" I thought. It all became clear, however, as my eyes were quickly drawn to the unused needles strewn across our bed. Questions rushed through my mind like a flood: "How did she find them?" "What am I going to say?" "How far will I go?" "How can I get out of this?" Interrupting my stream of thoughts, Christelle said in disbelief, "What is this?"

I confessed to using performance-enhancing drugs (steroids), and that led to a barrage of many other questions regarding alcohol, pornography, and our marriage. I had a choice to make: would I come clean and reveal all I'd hidden from my wife, or would I tell only half-truths, revealing only what I wanted? The bleak state of our lives was sinking in, the fog of deception lifting. "What do I really want?" I asked myself. Did I want this marriage? Did I want to continue leading my marriage and ministry in the shadows of hiddenness? Or did I want what I set out to have—a prospering marriage and a life fully given to God? Could I even have that if I wanted it at this point? I had to decide, and decide quickly.

I (Christelle) sat stunned as the situation began to unfold and hidden things came to light. I knew God had tried to prepare me, but I didn't feel ready to hear Antonio's confession. I sat in disbelief as he spoke, and I felt the heat of anger coupled with the pain of hurt rise within me. My words came out like swords, slashing and cutting Antonio with each blow. "How could this be?" I thought. "We had the perfect life!" That night reality hit me in the face and I also had a choice to make.

A slew of probing, endless questions came at me (Antonio), and each one was warranted. The interrogation was rapid fire and gave me no chance to lie. Christelle was devastated, but it would be weeks before I'd feel the weight of my sin, betrayal, and compromise. I was self-deceived—looking through the eyes of selfishness and self-gratification.

God had us right where He wanted us, however—a place where He could expose the compromise penetrating our home and destroying us from the inside. He desired the best for us—a life full of purpose and destiny. But little did we realize this storm was just the vehicle to get us there.

The following days were some of the hardest we've ever had, but we felt God's grace upon our lives. He gave us a plan, and much of what we learned and implemented during that time is woven throughout this book.

The pinnacle of sin is not reached by one decision or choice, but rather by a series of choices. That was true in our situation—a lot of little things brought us to our moment of crisis. Deep down we wanted our marriage, and in the days that followed we decided to fight for our union and do whatever it took to not only survive but thrive. God sent many people to help us, including Bob and Audrey Meisner of *My New Day* and various prayer ministries. But, more than anything else, we stuck together, persevered, and day by day things began to change.

Little steps became big strides. We went from hopelessness and despair to being grateful for a flourishing marriage. A desire to share the principles behind this transformation and help others is the reason we wrote this book.

THE ATTACKS ARE REAL

What if we told you our homes and marriages are regularly attacked, yet we have little to no defense, let alone an offense, to protect ourselves? What if the culture itself and the spirit of this age are the very things destroying our families, and the possibilities of future generations, from the inside? What if we defined some of those attacks and also provided strategies for defending our homes and protecting our lineage? Would you heed the warnings? Would you destroy the things that have infiltrated your household, such as wrong worldviews, ideas, and practices?

God calls us in First Peter 5:8 to *"be alert and of sober mind. Your enemy the devil prowls around like a roaring lion looking for someone to devour"* (NIV). We must be aware of how the enemy operates, the strategies he employs, and the avenues he takes. There is a war in our homes, whether we realize it or not—it's not fake or made up. Many, we fear, want to pretend like nothing is happening and no harm will come near. Our desire is to make you aware of the enemy's tactics and share some of the protections we can have and ways we can build a strong marriage and a thriving home.

We speak to many people who possess this as the ultimate desire for their family—a home on fire for God and the many wonderful blessings He has for them. No victory happens by coincidence, however, and nothing worthwhile is left to chance. Every marriage and family is worth fighting for in a deliberate manner. God gives us answers to this culture's ever-increasing bombardment of lies. We don't have to be content with the status quo when God wants to give us so much more.

A Call to Arms

We must have desperation in our lives and draw a line we won't allow the enemy to cross. A call to arms is not figurative but literal and pertinent because we're in a real war. The attack is coming from every direction, gunfire from every side. Fighter pilots are taking aim from the air, dropping bombs on cities and homes. Tanks of sexual immorality, discontentment, and divorce are slowly pushing their way into our marriages, while seaborne invasions of tolerance of sin, apathy, and lust are threatening our children.

Our attitude must be similar to that of Winston Churchill when he famously declared before the advent of World War II: "You ask, what is our policy? I will say: it is to wage war, by sea, land, and air, with all our might and with all the strength that God can give us; to wage war...that is our policy. You ask, what is our aim? I can answer in one word: It is victory, victory at all costs, victory in spite of all terror, victory, however long and hard the road may be; for without victory, there is no survival."[1]

The battlefront is our homes, and the enemy's weapons of warfare are ideas and values that have permeated our society. These godless ideas have completely saturated our lives and created ungodly cultural norms only visible when we compare them with Scripture. We must look at each norm individually and ask, "Where did this idea come from and how did we let it in?"

The Culture

Let's begin by considering the word culture, which is "a particular form of a civilization, a certain nation or period. It is the development of the mind by education or training. The behaviors and belief characteristics of a particular social, ethnic, or age group."[2]

A culture is a learned set of ideas, behaviors, values, and beliefs that are shared by a group of people. Everything around us has a culture that includes expressions, habits, and activities a group of people view as normal. Churches, schools, employers, and sports teams all have distinct cultures setting them apart from each other. Many things contribute to a certain culture—friends, family, education, songs, TV shows, clothing, neighborhood characteristics, and the list goes on and on.

We must begin by viewing the cultural foundation we as parents have allowed in our homes. Others can influence our families, but only because we allow them to do so. By not objecting or participating ourselves, we have given a green light to patterns of thinking or ways of speaking in our homes. We have allowed the culture of our homes to be influenced from the outside because we have not been active in setting the culture ourselves.

FIERCE DETERMINATION

My older brother, sister, and I attended public school until I was in seventh grade, my older brother was in ninth, and my sister in fifth. After that year, I never attended another public school again. My mother saw a pattern of lifestyle decisions her children were making and was troubled enough to take us out of public school. The friends and influences we were being faced with were infiltrating her children. She was not going to allow the outside culture to determine the state of her home. There was sin and compromise in her children, and she became a mother bear protecting her cubs. We cleaned out our lockers at the end of the year and said goodbye to our friends, not knowing if we would ever see them again.

My mother was fierce in protecting her children, which I now see as love. At the time I didn't understand some of the decisions she made, but now I see she was demonstrating good parenting skills through leading and caring for her children. She loved us so much she wouldn't allow someone else to dictate the culture and lifestyle of her home. She realized the hard way that what influences her kids in their formative years shapes their lives.

The next year we started homeschooling, and later we went to private school. We began studying the Bible and attending prayer meetings regularly—our home culture and worldview started changing. This is the attitude we should have toward anything in our home and family that is hostile toward God's values. To this day I am so thankful for the protection and hope for my future because of my parents' proactive decisions.

We know this may be a different way of looking at things many are not used to. Some may contest that children need to make their own decisions or experience what is out there in the world so they aren't shocked later in life. However, after we share some facts about where we're going as a culture and society today, we urge you to consider soberly and seriously what you'll allow to influence the culture of your home.

If you have any Trojan horses infiltrating from the inside, it might be time to kick them out. Some of us have made peace treaties, allowing certain influences inside the walls of our dwellings. These might include friends, schools, forms of media, and even other family members. We need to decide if it's time to aggressively change the direction of our households.

WHAT THE CULTURE IS SAYING

Please don't be fooled by what the culture around us is saying. It doesn't suggest secular ideologies, but rather screams and enforces them by bombarding our minds through TV, movies, friends, education, and music, which is one of the greatest tools of all. Andrew Fletcher, a politician and a writer from the 1700s, said, "If a man were permitted to make all the ballads, he need not care who should make the laws of a nation."[3] Music is one of the quickest and easiest ways for people to learn worldviews. It has increasingly become a major method to rapidly create and spread cultural norms and ideologies throughout the world.

The infiltration of culture is a very real thing. We now have many widespread and unbiblical "norms." But where did these come from? Why do we believe they are true? We wish to challenge the status quo in a culture that is secular, full of lies, and contrary to God's ways. The following are some of the cultural "norms" dealing specifically with marriage and family:

- A parent is considered a legalist or stifling their children if they make rules and expect them to be followed.

- Parents have made providing a good education as the number one goal in raising their children.

- Our children can and should be missionaries in their secular schools.

- It's okay for girls to pursue boys.

- Eighteen years old is considered an adult.

- Date your way to a mate and eventually one will stick.

- A young adult should finish secondary education before getting married.

- Parents don't need to be involved in their kid's decision about whom to marry.

- I can only afford to have one or two children.

- I can fall out of love with my spouse.

The main issue with these norms is that God's ways are contrary to these ideas. These ideas were developed out of a humanistic worldview rather than out of an understanding of the Word of God. We have too often followed the idea, "When in Rome, do as the Romans do."[4] The scary part is that most of us don't even know where we get these worldviews. We just value them and live them out instinctively. We've created a Christianity that conforms to our culture rather than defining our way of life from the Bible first and then developing the culture of our homes.

We won't speak to every one of the concepts listed above, as each one could be a book itself. Throughout this book, we'll try to discuss many of these topics in some way while making you aware of the origins of these cultural ideas. There are other alarming hot button topics—such as abortion and homosexual unions—that are also affecting the home, which we have excluded so as not to distract from the focus of igniting a fire for God that will never go out.

Romans 12:2 says in the Amplified Version:

> *Do not be conformed to this world (this age), [fashioned after and adapted to its external, superficial customs], but be transformed (changed) by the [entire] renewal of your mind [by its new ideals and its new attitude], so that you may prove [for yourselves] what is the good and acceptable and perfect will of God, even the thing which is good and acceptable and perfect [in His sight for you].*

We want to speak to and question the status quo of what the culture is saying today. Our hope is to bring light through biblical truth to expose the lies hidden in the darkness. We believe that as you study the Scriptures and compare them to the current issues we're facing, you'll find truth and clearly see that many of our humanistic cultural ideologies need complete reformation.

For many young people, the concepts listed above are second nature and completely normal—they don't even think they need discussion. They're a part of life and "they are what they are." What many fail to see is that these issues and cultural norms are due to a perspective imbedded in a person's overall worldview. We have forsaken the fundamental Christian worldview—surrounding marriage, family, and biblical ideals—and replaced them with secular and ungodly perspectives. These concepts have slowly crept into our society through various influences, creating "norms" in the home and church. What's worse is that many in our culture have been conditioned to sift all ideas through the strainer of relativism, tolerance, and philosophical diversity.

This generation is bombarded with humanist and feminist philosophies in the schools they attend, the movies they watch, the music they listen to, the magazines they see, and even in the churches they attend. Men and women are taught self-indulgence, self-service, self-gratification, and a false happiness. On top of all that, one is more likely to hear false clichés, such as "that may be true for you, but it's not necessarily true for me."

The culture teaches people to view singleness as merely a time to "try out" different girls and guys romantically, instead of preparing themselves for one of the greatest gifts God has given us—marriage and raising a family. Some of the richest blessings we'll ever experience are found in a godly marriage and in raising children to be wholehearted followers of Jesus Christ. The dating game, however, is nothing more than practicing for divorce. Our children are giving away their emotions and physical bodies when these belong to one person—their spouse.

When you look at the issues and pressures facing young people today, one of the biggest questions is, "Where are the parents?" Voddie T. Baucham Jr., in his book *Family Driven Faith*, says, "Unless your child is wiser than Solomon, stronger than Samson, and more godly than David (all of whom sinned sexually), they are susceptible to sexual sin, and these premature relationships serve as open invitations."[5] He goes on to say, "Being involved in such exclusive relationships before you are ready to be married is like going shopping without any money; either you will leave frustrated, or you will take something that doesn't belong to you."[6] Another wrong worldview confronting young people in Western societies is that when a person turns 18, he or she has reached adulthood. When a person turns 18 in our culture, they usually begin making all the decisions for their lives. They can date the person they want, stay out as late as they want, take the job they want, and work as much as they want (or not); and no one should, nor has the right to, say anything against their decisions.

I (Antonio) remember sitting down with a young man in his early 20s who was interested in a young woman. The parents of the woman wanted to be involved in the courting aspect of their relationship—the guy wanted none of it. He told the young lady, "You are old enough to make your own decisions and they don't have a right to say anything." It was like he was saying that all of the years of caring, protecting, training, and nurturing from the parents should be dismissed by the magical age of 18. Then, some stranger, who hasn't been a part of her life, has major influence and an even greater wisdom to impart than the people who have raised her. This is nonsense!

WHERE DID THIS COME FROM?

Where did we get such thinking, and who taught it to us? Let's look at what the Bible says: *"Therefore a man shall leave his father and mother and be joined to his wife, and they shall become one flesh"* (Gen. 2:24).

From the very beginning of time, sons and daughters were meant to be under the covering of their parents until the day they got married. Having said this, we know the questions this statement might raise: "What if I never marry?" "What if my parents don't care?" "What if my parents are not Christian believers?" or "Don't young people have to learn to make their own decisions?" The questions vary because of the different backgrounds of the people involved. We will answer these questions more extensively later on, but here's a story that will help address this issue.

Recently we had the privilege of providing pre-marital counseling for a great couple from Sweden. Joakim and Hanna have incredible personal testimonies with a deep love for one another. They asked us to counsel them while they were with us in Canada, as they were going back home in several months and hoping to get married. Some of our first sessions had to do with their parental involvement. We strongly suggested they speak to their parents and invite them to be a part of the relationship process, asking them to speak into the relationship with regard to timing and more.

In Sweden, people don't typically ask permission from parents about whom they will date, let alone whom they will marry. A parent would actually be surprised if a guy asked a young lady's parents if he could go on a date with their daughter. They would think it odd. Guys don't even ask the father's permission to ask for his daughter's hand in marriage. The parents have nothing to do with the process, and, even if the parents didn't like their child's choice, not many kids would respect their opinion.

Where did this mindset originate? For some Americans and Canadians, this Swedish culture is probably difficult to understand, or maybe this makes total sense to some of us. However, some of our mindsets and ways of leading our homes are unbiblical. Leaving parents out of the relationship process is a growing problem and an area of compromise for many parents and young people alike.

PARENTAL INVOLVEMENT

In May 2013, during our Pursuit Internship School, we invited about 30 young adults to our home. They had a lot of questions about being single and choosing a future mate. Many of those in attendance were single with an average age of 20. We spoke with them for two hours, followed by another two hours of questions and answers. One of the main discussion points was about honoring one's parents.

In Ephesians 6:2, Paul encourages children to honor their parents, quoting from the Old Testament—*"Honor your father and mother,' which is the first commandment with promise"* (Eph. 6:2)—and this is reinforced in Colossians 3:20 where it says, *"Children, obey your parents in all things."* We strongly encourage young ladies and men to include their parents in the whole dating process, not merely at the end as a formality. They should be heavily involved in the process from the very start. However, some have ceded authority to their children, even in their kids' early teens.

In Genesis 2:24, God sets a standard that *"a man shall leave his father and mother and be joined to his wife, and they shall become one flesh."* A son leaves his parents to live with his wife while the young lady leaves her parents' home and comes under her husband's covering. Parents should be involved in the courtship process until the young couple gets married. Not only are parents the covering over their children until the time they marry, but they also have the right to veto who's involved in the child's life and potentially whom he or she will marry.

We don't believe a child should leave that covering and protection of their home until they get married—unless for an internship, university, or a similar pursuit. Leaving parental covering is not justified merely because a young person has some money and can afford to move out and live with a roommate. We realize this is a broad statement, and there are older singles who may eventually choose to leave home and who will perhaps never marry. What we see as a pattern, however, is that someone turns 18 and then thinks they have the right to move out and be on their own, as if they are fully trained and now ready to leave the nest. Parents assume, for the most part, that this is when the responsibility for raising their children ends.

This simply isn't true, however, because parents should be helping and supporting some of the most important decisions their child will be making in the years leading up to marriage. There's also great promises and blessing for children as they choose to honor their parents by including them in this decision-making process.

God commands us to honor our father and mother, whether or not they are saved. He doesn't qualify that statement other than to say "it will go well with you" (see Eph. 6:3). The most important decision of our life is following Jesus, and the second is choosing a mate. In most cases, even the unsaved parents know the young adult better than anyone else and can sense if there's something wrong with the relationship. More than likely, the parents will ask questions their child may not have thought about before.

Proverbs 15:22 tells us, *"Plans fail for lack of counsel, but with many advisers they succeed"* (NIV). If the parents of a young adult couple are deceased or not Christians, we suggest they ask a godly couple to mentor them and speak into their lives. If a parent gives advice contrary to Scripture, then the Word of God must have final authority, but the parent should still be treated with honor.

"KNOT YET" TREND

In our current culture, for a variety of reasons, people are getting married later and later in life. Studies show that "one of the most important social developments of our time is the recent rise in age at first marriage, which now stands at 27 for women and 29 for men, a historic high."[7] There are a variety of reasons for this trend and varying degrees of consequences.

The high value placed on education and the possibility for better income is one of the main reasons for marrying so late in life. Carol Morello, from *The Washington Post,* wrote, "Everyone is pushing marriage to their late 20s and early 30s, the Wal-Mart cashier as well as the Wells Fargo executive, but the Wells Fargo executive is getting married in her late 20s and having her first child in her early 30s. The Wal-Mart checkout guy is having his first kid in his early 20s, and often marries in his late 20s, often to someone who is not the mother of his first child."[8]

Another startling fact is that, "According to U.S. Census, 48% of U.S. mothers giving birth for the first time were unmarried."[9]

The normal reality for a lot of women is that they will have their first child before their first marriage.[10] In today's culture, marriage, sex, and children are not connected to each other as they were in the past. Singles are using their time to date, socialize, and have sex. People are sexually active whether or not they are married and are using birth control and abortion as a means of ensuring the prevention of children.

Men are learning more about cohabitation rather than leading a family. By waiting to marry, women will make more money but leave behind some of their best years for raising children—that is, if they even choose to have one. Money and education are now more valuable than a great marriage or raising a family. We aren't saying that getting an education and using wisdom about marriage timing is wrong. Getting a good education is great and should be pursued. It just shouldn't be the first priority we teach and train our kids about. Rather, our values and focus should be on the Lord and His ways.

The lines between marital fulfillment, marital stability, and potential financial earnings are a real tug-of-war. Karen Swallow Prior confirms this by writing, "Young adults are taking longer to finish their education and stabilize their work lives. Culturally, young adults have increasingly come to see marriage as a 'capstone' rather than a 'cornerstone'—that is, something they do after they have all their other ducks in a row, rather than a foundation for launching into adulthood and parenthood."[11]

Patricia H. Shiono, the director of research and grants for epidemiology at the Center for the Future of Children, states:

> Demographers point to several societal events that have had major impacts on divorce rates. Divorce rates increased after every major war, decreased during

the Great Depression, and decreased during the post-World War II economic boom. The large increase in divorce rates in the 1970s was bolstered by the introduction of no-fault divorce laws, the reduction in fertility as a result of improved methods of contraception, and the legalization of abortion. However, most scholars believe that the single most important social change that made divorce possible was the increase in the employment of women and the corresponding economic independence that employment provided.[12]

The more self-serving we become, the less marriage and family become the focus. During the Great Depression, couples tended to stay together. What other choice did they have? Those who grew up in the United States during the deprivation of the Great Depression and went on to fight in World War II are considered the "Great Generation." Through the struggles of life, this generation fought together in a unified and sacrificial manner. We need such an attitude today more than ever before.

In a radio interview, Albert Mohler, who is the president of the Southern Baptist Theological Seminary, set off a firestorm when he said, "The sin that I think besets this generation…is the sin of delaying marriage as a lifestyle option among those who intend some day to get married but they just haven't yet."[13] Voddie Baucham Jr. expands on this by writing, "Some young adults have their own ideas, however, and believe there's experiences they need before they dive into the deep, dark, oppressive world of marriage. For some it may be traveling to Europe or Africa while others may want to first spend time on the mission field. Still others may believe there's some magic age at which one automatically becomes 'ready' for marriage. Whatever the case may be, it's a far cry from the biblical admonition, '*He who finds a wife finds a good thing and obtains favor from the Lord*' (Prov. 18:22)."[14]

It's our personal belief that people are marrying and having children later because of the work and sacrifice it requires of them. Money and prestige may seem better and far outweigh the effort required to invest in a marriage and family. As a drive-through generation, we can also have drive-through marriages and push back the responsibility of marriage until later in life because we see the price as too high. The feminist movement that gained momentum in the 1970s distorted marriage and family as "constricting, suffocating and an enemy to the liberated women's larger hopes."[15]

Germaine Greer, one of the main voices for the feminist movement, wrote in her book *The Female Eunuch* (first written in 1970):

> What does the average girl marry for? The answer will probably be made—love. Love can exist outside marriage—indeed for a long time it was supposed that it always did. Love can take many forms; why must it be exclusive? Security? Security is a chimera, especially if it is supposed to mean the preservation of a state of happy togetherness, which exists at the time of marriage. Should no obvious disasters like adultery or separation occur, people still change: neither partner will be, ultimately, the person who got married in the beginning.[16]

Many ideas from Greer's book and this movement are a great part of our current worldview. But we can barely see the light at the end of the tunnel for all the confusion these concepts create.

Gary Thomas, in his book *Sacred Marriage*, says, "Any situation that calls me to confront my selfishness has enormous spiritual value…and the real purpose of marriage may not be happiness as much as it is holiness."[17] Marriage kills selfishness. In addition, having children places your selfishness on the judge's stand where the guilty verdict is passed; it allows you to die to self slowly but ever so aggressively. With each child, more self dies, and when you didn't think you had more to kill, you find out that you still do. Through the process, God reveals the glory of being a father or a mother and the mystery of marriage. The purpose of marriage isn't to kill selfishness from our lives, but it is part of the process. It is designed for enjoyment, friendship, partnership, procreation, and to become Christlike. Gary Thomas again says, "If the purpose of marriage was simply to enjoy an infatuation and make me 'happy,' then I'd have to get a 'new' marriage every two or three years."[18]

CLEAR, BOLD, AND HONEST

Christelle and I are passionate about having a biblical worldview and lives that reflect godly character. It doesn't matter if something is "normal" in our culture today if it opposes God and doesn't bring forth fruit in our lives. Our zeal comes from our own personal heartaches and triumphs, from the defeats and victories of our own lives. So much regret could have been prevented. We're passionate because of the mediocre lives we have lived.

The correlation between the diets of influences we ingested and the disastrous results we received were no coincidence. We were in desperate need of revival, and God met us right where we were. God called us to a lifestyle only possible with Him.

In June 2008, a few short weeks after that dramatic day in our bedroom, we took a trip to Kansas City to visit family and take some much-needed time off. During that trip we visited the International House of Prayer, a 24/7 prayer and worship ministry continuing nonstop since 1999. We weren't prepared for what God was about to do in our lives.

Waking up with flu-like symptoms, I (Antonio) wasn't eager to sit through the morning's two-hour prayer meeting. Christelle, however, had already booked a prophetic ministry time for us, so we decided to spend some time in the prayer room as we waited.

A few minutes into the meeting felt like an eternity. I looked at my watch, "How am I ever going to get through two hours?" I thought. All this waiting was for "prophetic ministry," and "What was that about, anyway?" My anxiety and skepticism grew. Surprisingly, the worship was pretty good, and then halfway through the session the prayer leader invited whomever was sick to stand up for prayer. After a nudge from Christelle, I hesitantly stood and a group of people gathered around me and prayed.

One guy stayed after the others left.

What he said marked my life forever. "I see you walking a clear, bold, and honest walk in the spirit of Joel 2," he said. I looked up and he was gone. "He must be crazy," I thought. Although I had very little experience with prophecy, I knew he was saying something I wasn't living. My life so far had the opposite track record. I'm so thankful, however, that God has an unusual editing process. At this point in our restoration, I had truly repented of my previous lifestyle, but I didn't recognize that God now saw me in a completely different light. I just thought that guy was out to lunch.

Two hours later we entered into the room for prophetic ministry. Three young people were assigned to pray for Christelle and me, and all three of them sat across from us. One of the young men appeared to be 15 years old, and so my expectations of him were small. I wanted experienced and mature Christians ministering to us. What he said, however, changed the direction of our home forever. "I see you walking a clear, bold, and honest walk in the spirit of Joel chapter 2," he declared.

What? I was floored! How could this young man say word for word what the other had said just hours before? I suddenly realized *God* was speaking to me. The weight of those words hit my heart with intensity. From that day forward, I was called to live out a *clear, bold, and honest walk*—and to call many others to that type of walk as well. I knew God had a plan, even though I didn't know how this would happen.

A WHOLEHEARTED PURSUIT

"Now, therefore," says the Lord, "turn to Me with all your heart, with fasting, with weeping, and with mourning." So rend your heart, and not your garments; return to the Lord your God, for He is gracious and merciful, slow to anger, and of great kindness; and He relents from doing harm. Who knows if He will turn and relent, and leave a blessing behind Him? ...Blow the trumpet in Zion, consecrate a fast, call a sacred assembly; gather the people, sanctify the congregation, assemble the elders, gather the children and nursing babes. ... Let the priests...weep between the porch and the altar; let them say, "Spare Your people, O Lord" (Joel 2:12-17).

In this passage, God gives us the key to receiving His mercy and deliverance—turn to Him wholeheartedly. In a time of crisis, the Lord requires His people to return to Him completely with prayer, fasting, and a rending of their hearts—with a concern for what's happening on the inside of them rather than just what's occurring in their external lives. We did this in our lives and marriage, and this decision transformed the direction of our home.

The prophetic words given me in the prayer room that day were for more people than just me. They were a call to every home and family that wants revival in their midst. We desperately need God's help if this is going to become a reality in our homes. As we do our part in rending our hearts and turning to Him in humility, He will release His supernatural power and grace.

In Joel's day, people tore their garments to show their grief and desperation. However, what God desires is the tearing of our heart, which speaks of dealing radically with the matters of our internal life. God is more interested in what is taking place in our hearts rather than our outward appearances and behaviors. We are not talking about outer religious activities, but rather an inward turning that affects outer realities.

To *rend* means to tear something violently or forcibly. We need to tear our hearts away from everything in our lives quenching the Spirit of God. Speaking symbolically of this tearing, or radical obedience, Jesus spoke of spiritual violence in the book of Matthew: *"If your right eye causes you to sin, pluck it out...for it is more profitable for you that one of your members perish, than for your whole body to be cast into hell"* (Matt. 5:29).

Tearing our heart is intensely personal and painful. Some want the Spirit to free them from sinful patterns and relationships without requiring any personal choices or heart-rending changes. But we cannot pursue wholeheartedness in a casual way. Some hope for a process that is gentle and easy, but there's no such thing. Living in an ordinary manner is not what's needed for the times we live in. Extreme times require extreme measures!

I (Antonio) walked this out even though I was immature and weak in areas. I began leading prayer meetings and Bible studies in my home for my wife and children, even though I really didn't know how. We asked God what media to remove and felt led to cut cable and cleanse our home of movies that were quenching our new God-breathed and fasted lifestyles. For a whole year we didn't watch any form of entertainment. It wasn't easy, but we needed to remove from our life all habits inhibiting growth in godliness. We also cleaned out all secular music and only had worship music in our home 24 hours a day. This was the beginning of a lifestyle we still follow today. Choices that once seemed difficult have become vital so we can walk in all the Lord has for us.

Since that season of transformation began, we now have limited media intake in our lives, with our choices focused on the quality of the content. We've experienced God's life-changing power in such a way that nothing else matters. The enticements of movies, music, and various forms of entertainment have lost their luster. We've tasted God, and now nothing else compares. The static that once filled the spiritual airwaves of our personal lives and home is now gone and He can speak to us and work freely.

We invite you to embrace a Joel 2 lifestyle, with a heart turned to God in every area of your life. The history we make is hinged upon our hearts turning. We can't continue in the same direction we're going. Where there is no hope, He gives a remedy. The answer is turning to Him with all of our hearts. It's a holy invitation to fast and pray—*a Joel 2 cry is sounding.* Our hope can't be in the government, a ministry, or a church; nor can it be in any man. It must be in the Lord, and we need Heaven to release power upon our homes today. Just like God revealed His great mercy and grace to our family, He now stands and extends that same invitation to you. Will you take it?

Chapter 2

ESTABLISHING FOUNDATIONS

The perfect marriage is a uniting of three persons—a man and a woman and God. That is what makes marriage holy.
—BILLY GRAHAM, *Day by Day**

When we were a young married couple, both only 20 years old, we received the news that Christelle was pregnant with our first child. Our excitement was uncontainable! We were ecstatic about this new adventure we were embarking on. However, the reality was that we had no idea what we were doing as new parents. At the time we lived in Minneapolis, Minnesota, and we were all alone—one set of parents lived in Boca Raton, Florida, and the other in Kona, Hawaii.

We entered into this new season of our marriage knowing some basic concepts of childrearing but without any real understanding of what parenting was all about. In fact, we began our parenting journey not really knowing what *marriage* was all about. Although we had great hopes for our marriage relationship, the truth was that our marriage was pretty rocky. Of all the young couples out there, *we* weren't supposed to have a rocky marriage; we were both blessed with a rich, secure family heritage. Despite our strong Christian upbringing, we made many mistakes. But God had a plan.

Seemingly out of nowhere, we were given an opportunity to attend 12 weeks of classes on supernatural childbirth. We thought we were going to learn about childbirth and raising children, but instead what we learned was how to have a godly home, how to pray, how to read the Word together, and how to live in intimacy. We barely touched on the topic we thought we would be learning about, but we really studied the scriptural blueprint that God has for a beautiful and successful marriage. We learned so many valuable lessons during that time—lessons that are still bearing fruit in our lives to this day.

Over the years, we have listened to countless stories of marriages in crisis. Not only that, but our own marriage has been tested many times. We have seen that the natural human tendency is to remedy the problem as quickly as possible. Married couples in trouble often look into improving their communication skills, their sex lives, rescheduling their priorities, and so on. While all of that can be good and beneficial, the real problems run much deeper than that.

We have to learn what it means for a man to *leave* his father and mother and *cleave* to his wife, what a *covenant* is, and what it means to be *one flesh*. This is essential to successive generations of strong marriages.

THE PURPOSE OF MARRIAGE

Derek Prince writes, "Adam did not think up marriage. He did not even know he needed a wife. Marriage originated in the mind of God. God established the very purpose for marriage; He founded all the rules for it, as well as the fruit."[1] God Himself is the One who thought up marriage. The ways of the Kingdom were established in the family, with a father and a mother, a bridegroom and a bride, sons and daughters, all serving together in unity as a family unit.

One of the main reasons God established marriage was for His glory. It is not a contract but a covenant relationship to be entered into—a unity between friends. Marriage begins and ends in friendship. Without friendship, all we really have in marriage are business partners who live together. And without friendship, a marriage simply will not last through the storms of life.

The writer of Ecclesiastes speaks to this issue:

> *Two are better than one, because they have a good reward for their labor. For if they fall, one will lift up his companion. But woe to him who is alone when he falls, for he has no one to help him up. Again, if two lie down together, they will keep warm; but how can one be warm alone? Though one may be overpowered by another, two can withstand him. And a threefold cord is not quickly broken* (Ecclesiastes 4:9-12).

These verses speak to the need for companionship, first and foremost. Two are better than one because they have a good reward for their labor; in other words, their covenant relationship is rewarded. The threefold cord described in this passage is the three-fold covenant bond that unites God with the husband and wife. This is covenant marriage relationship.

Solomon gives three reasons why friendship or companionship is a source of strength. First, when we fall, our companion will help us up again; second, if two lie together, they will keep warm; and third, if two are attacked, together they can overcome. A strand of three cords is not easily broken! God designed covenant relationships so we can learn how to give each other the advantage, and not take advantage for ourselves. This is giving, not taking. It is in the giving of ourselves that we are fulfilled. This is the greatest part of marriage.

Understanding unity is vital to establishing longevity in marriage. When we have not been in unity, we were not serving, working for, or thinking of each other but ourselves. This is a fierce struggle, but the only way to have a great marriage. Our aim must be oneness in all that we do. This is why Genesis states, *"Therefore a man shall leave his father and mother and be joined to his wife, and they shall become one flesh"* (Gen. 2:24).

Gary Chapman explains that "one flesh" in Genesis 2:24 is the "same Hebrew word used of God Himself in Deuteronomy 6:4, where we read, 'Hear, O Israel: The Lord our God, the Lord is one!' The word 'one' speaks of composite unity as opposed to absolute unity. The Scriptures reveal God to be Father, Son and Spirit, yet one. We do not have three Gods but one God, triune in nature."[2] Likewise, in marriage, this is a similar picture, where two become one flesh and then become one spirit with God. In marriage God binds two people together and positions them as one in Him, continually bringing them into greater unity with each other and with Himself.

A COVENANT VERSUS A CONTRACT

An older friend of ours, whom we dearly love, recently lost his wife to cancer. While celebrating her life, he said something that struck us deeply: "My days are so long without my wife, because they are without her." The Bible makes it clear that there is only one foundation for true unity between human beings, whether they are men or women. That foundation is covenant. The nature of covenant is one of the most beautiful, jealously guarded secrets of the Kingdom of God. And we believe it's a pearl of His heart.

A covenant has several components to it. It is the most binding form of agreement between two parties that involves the exchange of strengths for weaknesses. Marriages are covenant relationships because they are designed to operate based on this exchange. An understanding of covenant is so needed in our lives today. Most young people we speak to have no clue what we are talking about when we talk about this subject. When we even say the word "covenant," they respond by saying, "A what?" as if we were speaking a different language.

A covenant is a pledge or vow between two people to carry out the terms agreed upon. The blood covenant is the strongest agreement known to man, for no lasting relationship can be built without a covenant. In Abraham's time, the blood covenant symbolized an unbreakable bond that was honored until the time of death.

Certain signs or tokens are given within a covenant that signify the agreement between the husband and wife. For example, when God made a covenant with Noah after the flood, the rainbow was the token or sign of that covenant (see Gen. 9:11-17). In Abraham's time, every male child had to be circumcised as a token of the covenant between God and His people. Since the cross, circumcision of the heart, which is an inward working of the Holy Spirit, is a sign of the covenant relationship we have with God. And in the marriage covenant, the wearing of wedding bands is an outward sign of an inward commitment to each other as husband and wife.

In his book *Husbands and Fathers*, Derek Prince says, "The key to marriage is two words: leave and cleave. If you do not leave, you cannot cleave. If you are not willing to step out of the parental background and make a new start, you will never achieve true unity with your spouse."[3] We would add that if you have troubled times in your marriage, the steps to restoration are the same: cleave to your spouse, never separating or allowing distance between you. God wants marriages to stay together as one flesh. We were not meant to live our lives being *separated from* each other, but rather *uncovered before* one another. (It should be noted here that we are not recommending this for abusive situations.)

What we are describing here is a marriage of transparency where husband and wife know each other's strengths, weaknesses, vulnerabilities, victories, and defeats. A side-by-side marriage is unsatisfying and self-preserving. A covenantal, friendship-based, face-to-face marriage is what God intended marriage to be—a covenant between a man and woman, and before God.

A CONTRACT

Marriage has been largely distorted through the simple fact that divorce is so accessible and so common in our day and age. Marriage today is often looked upon as a contract rather than a covenant. Chapman goes on to write, "According to Christian researcher George Barna, 25 percent of what he calls 'born again' Christians—those who have accepted Jesus Christ as Savior and Lord—have experienced a divorce. Worse, 23 percent—nearly a quarter—have been divorced more than once!"[4] So it really doesn't make much of a difference whether we are speaking to Christians or non-Christians, the divorce statistics are very similar. This happens when marriage is defined in terms of a human contractual agreement instead of a God-ordained covenant.

Because marriage has largely been entered into as a contract rather than a covenant, societal values have steadily declined. We would argue that we don't have a sexual immorality problem, or a divorce problem, or a family problem in our culture—we have a marriage problem! Our society has a deficit in understanding and implementing the marriage covenant.

Gary Thomas writes, "In a man-centered view, we will maintain our marriage as a long as our earthly comforts, desires, and expectations are met. In a God-centered view, we preserve our marriage because it brings glory to God and points a sinful world to a reconciling Creator."[5] And Andreas Kostenberger goes on to point out in his book, *God, Marriage, and Family*, that a contract has five general characteristics:

1. They are typically made for a limited period of time.

2. They most often deal with specific actions.

3. They are conditional upon the continued performance of contractual obligations by the other partner.

4. They are entered into for one's own benefit.

5. They are sometimes unspoken and implicit.[6]

God hasn't called us to live in contracts with our spouse, but to establish a covenant in His sight.

THE MYSTERY OF COVENANT

Clearly, something has gone terribly wrong in our understanding of marriage. The divorce epidemic is everywhere. Marriage has been reduced to something far below the biblical ideal. It has become a distorted, superficial, humanistic contract, nothing more than a partnership with someone who lives with you. Sadly, this is true not only in secular circles but in much of the church as well.

The mystery of marriage will not be understood properly by the powers of our intellect. Understanding covenant comes only through revelation from God. He has to reveal to us the depths, soberness, and joy of the mystery of marriage. Andreas J. Kostenberger defines covenant like this: "Marriage covenant is defined as a sacred bond instituted by and publically entered into before God (whether or not this is acknowledged by the married couple), normally consummated by sexual intercourse."[7] He goes on to say, "Marriage is not only permanent, sacred, intimate, mutual; it is also exclusive (Gen. 2:22-25; 1 Cor. 7:2-5). This means that no other human relationship must interfere with the marriage commitment between husband and wife. For this reason our Lord treated sexual immorality of a married person (Matt. 19:9; including lustful thoughts, Matt. 5:28) with utmost seriousness. For this reason too, premarital sex is illegitimate, since it violates the exclusive claims of one's future spouse."[8]

Our covenant relationship has been tested with some of the hardest and most difficult challenges that a marriage can be tested with. So we aren't saying this without pain, but through pain. When we finally understood the mystery and power of covenant, however, our marriage perspective completely changed. We finally understood our marriage to be lifelong—to be for one another. Through the most difficult times, through the highs and lows—we are one!

Derek Prince goes on to write, "The relationship between a husband and a wife is beautifully illustrated by a parable through the relationship of the moon to the sun. The moon is the 'glory' of the sun. The moon has no glory of its own. Its only beauty comes from reflecting the radiance of the sun."[9] So the glory of a marriage that lives face to face reflects the glory of each other with the light of God. This is the way we are meant to live.

A husband and wife within a covenant marriage will know each other more deeply, and to a far greater extent, than they can be known in any other way or by anyone else.[10] God's ultimate purpose for marriage is that a man and a woman come to know each other, which is neither temporary nor static. It is not merely intellectual, as we normally understand knowledge. Nor is it merely sexual—you can *lay* sexually with a man or a woman but not truly *know* them. Knowing your spouse means completely, unreservedly opening up each other's personalities. It embraces every area—physical, emotional, intellectual, and spiritual. There is so much to know of the other person that it is also endless searching of each other.

The word for *intimacy* comes from the Latin word *intimus*, meaning "inner."[11] True intimacy in marriage, then, comes when a married couple can be completely transparent with each other. This intimacy is walking together as a couple unashamed, knowing each other as no one else does. In fact, it is the real reason everyone gets married to begin with. All people want to share their lives with someone else, knowing fully and being fully known. God put this desire within each one of us. Every aspect of man longs and is made for woman, and the same is true for woman.

In his book, *The Family You've Always Wanted*, Gary Chapman states, "The biblical book of Genesis shows God creating woman from a portion of man's rib. When the man awoke from a deep sleep and saw the woman that God had created He said, *'This is now bone of my bones and flesh of my flesh; she shall be called "woman," for she was taken out of man'* (Gen. 2:23 NIV)."[12] There she stood, another like him but with unique differences, more like him than anything he had seen, and yet obviously different—separate from him and yet related to him.

For many newlyweds, intimacy is the only aim in their relationship. Over the course of time in marriage, however, maintaining this intimacy seems so out of reach that we just settle. We are not meant to settle or live halfhearted lives. We are meant to give our all—all of our love and affections. We are meant to live wholeheartedly and intimately with another. And we are not truly satisfied until we do.

It took me (Antonio) a long time to realize that marriage was not meant to serve my own personal satisfaction in receiving, but that I would get the most satisfaction in giving myself to Christelle. Today's culture tells us that we should concentrate on getting as much as possible as quickly as possible, and quit if we aren't happy. The Bible, however, teaches us that we are more satisfied when we give, because it is better to give than to receive.

THE PROPHETIC NATURE OF MARRIAGE

A Christian marriage that takes on the character of God is a beautiful picture of our Bridegroom God and His bride. From the beginning of creation, God was a matchmaker. He initiated the whole idea of husband and wife. He began human history with a marriage when He took out the rib of Adam to make Eve, and they became *one flesh.* God knew what Adam needed, and He prepared Eve for Adam and presented Eve to him. "From Genesis to Revelation," writes Derek Prince in *God Is a Matchmaker,* "from the first act in Eden to the last act in the heavenlies, the central theme of human history is marriage. Throughout this unfolding drama, God Himself does not remain merely a remote spectator. It is He who initiates the action, and it is in Him that it comes to its climax. From beginning to end, He is totally and personally involved."[13]

To bridge this prophetic picture, God ends the book of Revelation with the marriage supper of the Lamb. In Revelation 19:6-9, Scripture reveals to us the prophetic significance of our earthly marriage and how it is only a reflection of His heart for us. It started as an engagement and it ends as a wedding; forever He will be the Bridegroom God and we as the church will be His bride.

In Ephesians 5:25 Paul says, *"Husbands, love your wives, just as Christ also loved the church and gave Himself for her."* The sacrificial, unselfish, passionate love that Christ holds and displays for His church is the same kind of love that a Christian husband has the opportunity and privilege to live out and lavish upon His wife.

On the other side, in Ephesians 5:24, Paul says, *"Therefore, just as the church is subject to Christ, so let the wives be to their own husbands in everything."* A Christian wife has a corresponding privilege to demonstrate, in her relationship with her husband, the same kind of reverential love that the church has for Christ. "Contemporary society has no time for attitudes such as these, which proceed from 'a life laid down'"[14] and submitted to one another.

LIVING IN ALIGNMENT

God has established government and leadership in the earth in many ways, but one of the most foundational is within marriage and the family. The Bible says, *"But I want you to know that the head of every man is Christ, the head of woman is man, and the head of Christ is God"* (1 Cor. 11:3). Following is a simple illustration by Derek Prince that puts into perspective for us how God designed the chain of authority within a marriage and family following the framework of First Corinthians 11:3:[15]

God the Father

Christ

The husband

The wife

Children

The above chart shows us how our relationships should be aligned. Christ relates up to the Father and down to man, the man relates up to Christ and down to his wife, and the wife shares both up to her husband and down to her children. This is not in any way condescending, but an authority structure from a biblical perspective. It creates protection, accountability, nurturing, growth, service, unity, and relationship. This is how God has created the best possible family. Without a proper understanding of God's design, marriage and family will be out of alignment.

Looking at God's structure for delegated authority changed our perspective. Before knowing this, I (Antonio) was okay if Christelle led spiritually—it didn't matter to me, at least in the area of spiritual leadership. However, I had other areas in my life where I maintained a "me man, you woman" mindset. God dealt with some of those things later on in our marriage. He was bringing alignment into our marriage one step at a time.

John Bevere states in *Honor's Reward*, "Husbands are the head of the home. Chauvinistic men didn't conjure this up; it's God's idea. It is impossible to have true peace and blessing in a home where a wife leads or dominates, where a husband is not respected as the head. On the contrary, when a woman of God values her husband as the leader of the home, she will receive the reward of honor. It may come directly through him, but sometimes it can come by other avenues."[16]

We can find excuses for how not to live like this. It is easy to focus on how our spouse is not leading or not serving or not following the flow of God's authority structure. As we have discovered in our own marriage, it is wise and biblical to honestly examine yourself instead of your spouse. It's easy to look at your spouse and find their weakness and failures and point them out. But it is much harder to look at our own heart and motivations. We are held responsible for the light that we have been given and to walk with integrity in what God shows us for our own lives. To do otherwise is to assume a posture of judgment and pride rather than humility.

We would encourage you to walk in humility rather than pride, in love rather than judgment. Even as you read this, ask God to reveal your own heart, to bring to light things in your own life where you have operated in rebellion or pride in any way. God may reveal an attitude, words muttered under your breath, or wrong motives. It is God's kindness that leads us to repentance and true joy and freedom.

DEFINING THE ROLES

When we set out to marry, we have great dreams and aspirations of what our marriage will look like. As the years go by, it is not uncommon to be content with the mundaneness of life, letting go of those things we did at first and those dreams that we dreamed together in the beginning. For us to live out all God intended for us in marriage, we must have willing hearts that are ready for God to change us from within. To do this, we need more than just good intentions; we must understand what our distinctive roles are for a godly marriage.

Unfortunately, today's sitcoms, educational institutions, and self-driven "me" culture have painted a grossly distorted picture of what relationships and marriages are supposed to look like. For us to know how wrong this distorted picture really is, we need to look closely at how God meant for us to relate to one another as husband and wife. It is imperative that we correct our worldview until our entire view on life is a biblical one. What does God say in His Word about the roles of husband and wife?

THE ROLE OF THE HUSBAND (ANTONIO)

The roles of a man, husband, and father are so confused in our current culture that Christelle and I really felt we needed to clearly lay out God's original design. I will discuss in depth the role of a father in a later chapter, but for now I felt it necessary to clarify first what it means to be a man and a husband, because that is the foundation for godly fatherhood.

After God had made man from the dust of the ground and breathed into his nostrils the breath of life, He gave him some things to do: *"The Lord God took the man and put him in the Garden of Eden to tend and keep it"* (Gen. 2:15). The directive was clear with two words—to *tend* and to *keep*. Adam's initial mandate was to *tend* or to *work*, which means to cultivate, care for, manage, look after, and attend in making something grow. He was also to *keep* the Garden. The charge to *keep* implies that he was to guard, protect, and sustain the Garden that God had created. This is the starting point, the foundation, in knowing the role of a man.

Richard Phillips, in his powerful book *The Masculine Mandate*, writes, "Our calling in life really is this simple (although not therefore easy): We are to devote ourselves to working/building and keeping/protecting everything placed into our charge."[17] He goes on to write, "We are to invest our time, our energies, our ideas, and our passions in bringing good things into being. A faithful man, then, is one who has devoted himself to cultivating, building, and growing."[18] And again, "It is helpful, therefore, to see Genesis 2:15 'work' and 'keep' roles as separate but related. Two words that serve as good summaries of both terms are service and leadership."[19]

We as men are first responsible to serve and to protect. It almost sounds cliché, or like some kind of military motto, but this really is our mandate as men. To tend and to keep clearly defines every aspect of how we are to lead our lives, whether single or married. We cannot take this mandate lightly, and, if we have other worldviews, we must go back and consider what the Bible says regarding our mandate. We are not placed on this earth to take as much as possible for ourselves, but rather to serve, to protect, to guard, and to watch over, even to the point of giving our lives if we have to. Once we are married, this mandate continues on.

Paul went on to write:

> *Husbands, love your wives, just as Christ also loved the church and gave Himself for her, that He might sanctify and cleanse her with the washing of water by the word, that He might present her to Himself a glorious church, not having spot or wrinkle or any such thing, but that she should be holy and without*

blemish. So husbands ought to love their own wives as their own bodies; he who loves his wife loves himself (Ephesians 5:25-28).

Paul's words here clarify how a husband is to love his wife—he imitates what Jesus models. And the way Jesus loves is radical.

Jesus sacrificed His life for the church. He was beaten. He took responsibility and paid the price for transgressions that were not His own. He never defended Himself in any way. He gave extravagantly, sacrificed completely, and laid down His very life for you and for me. This is the way that Jesus loves—the example and model of how husbands are to love our wives.

Loving the way Jesus loves crushes all the myths of chauvinistic headship. Jesus led by taking on the very nature of a servant, in self-sacrificing leadership where He emptied Himself. This is how a husband is to lead and to love his wife and his family. The love of Christ is a sincere, pure, ardent, and constant affection. The greatness of His love for the church is evident in how He gave Himself unto death for it.

According to Ephesians 5:26, after Jesus loved the church so much that He gave Himself for her, He sanctified her and cleansed her with the washing of water by the word. How can we possibly follow Christ's example here? This may sound confusing to some. Some may even wonder, how do I sanctify and cleanse my wife? To *wash* means to bring a shower of refreshing, to bring cleansing by speaking the Word of God. God's Word brings newness inwardly and outwardly—this is not a one-time washing or speaking of the Word in your home, but a continual process that brings to mind the cleansing and consecration of water baptism; there is a regeneration of life and a renewed commitment to God. Daily commitment to my wife's spiritual growth should be my priority as well as hers.

Paul again says, *"However, each one of you also must love his wife as he loves himself, and the wife must respect her husband"* (Eph. 5:33 NIV). I have read this verse many times, but it wasn't until I read the book *Love and Respect* from Dr. Emerson Eggerichs that something clicked for me. He says, "God commands men to love their wives and wives to respect their husbands. This is not suggested but commanded. The most important part is that it's not only commanded but it's not conditional."[20] Men are to love their wives, period.

Tony Evans says regarding this:

> The biblical concept of *agape* love involves giving of yourself for the benefit of another, even at your own expense. Biblical love is defined by passionately and righteously seeking the well being of another. Biblical love is an act of the will and not just a fuzzy feeling in the stomach. That's why God commands us to love one another. Love really has nothing to do with whether you feel loving at a particular moment. It has to do with the need of the person being loved, not the feelings of the one doing the loving.[21]

My role as a husband in leading and loving my wife like Jesus loves the church is summarized like this: I am commanded to shower her with Jesus's self-sacrificing, self-denying, extravagant love—for her spiritual maturity. If my wife is lacking spiritual maturity, then that is a reflection of my leadership. In summary, my job as a husband is to tend and to keep my wife and my family. I am commanded to cultivate, nurture, and sustain the health and well-being of my home unto spiritual maturity. This is my God-given role as a husband. So is it for every husband who has ever lived and who will ever live. This is not optional but commanded.

THE ROLE OF THE WIFE (CHRISTELLE)

Wives, submit to your own husbands, as to the Lord.
For the husband is head of the wife, as also Christ is
head of the church; and He is the Savior of the body.
Therefore, just as the church is subject to Christ, so
let the wives be to their own husbands in everything...
and let the wife see that she respects her husband
(Ephesians 5:22-24,33).

It is hard for married women to know how to function in a healthy, thriving marriage without first knowing what we are created for. The very purpose as a wife is to be a helper and companion to our husband. But what is a helper?

And the Lord God said, "It is not good that man
should be alone; I will make him a **helper** *comparable*
to him" (Genesis 2:18 emphasis added).

To be a *helper* does not simply mean that we cook, clean, and take care of the domestic responsibilities, although we must not neglect those things. It is a far greater call than we can imagine, and holds the keys to great personal fulfillment and the outpouring of God's blessing in our lives. When a wife does not operate in this role, there is a continued restlessness in her soul and a discord within her marriage. When we refuse to honor God and walk in stubborn rebellion instead, we reject God's divine order. It only makes sense to have the most peace and fulfillment in doing the very thing we were created to do.

I agree with Tony Evans when he says:

The primary way that a wife helps her husband is to
help him become the leader that God has appointed

him to be. A wife ought to be her husband's chief fan, chief encourager, and chief support system. But she can't help her husband take the lead if she is constantly tearing him down or fighting him for control. In the Bible, a helper is someone who comes alongside another person to lift and build that person up. Jesus called the Holy Spirit our "Helper" in John 14:16. The Spirit's role is a good example of the way a helper works. Jesus said that the Spirit would not magnify Himself, but would glorify Jesus (John 16:13-14). ...The Spirit is co-equal in essence with the Father and the Son. He lost nothing of His deity when He became the Helper and took the role of glorifying Christ. This was a voluntary submission among spiritual equals, just as Christ's submission to the Father during His earthly ministry was a voluntary submission to accomplish the plan of redemption.[22]

The same is true of us as wives. We are called to come alongside our husbands by lifting him up. When we are a helper, the attitude we do this in is one of surrender, respect, and honoring in the way Jesus did. When we are truly helping, we do everything in submission to our husband and with respect for him and the role God positioned him in.

Problems arise when we want our husbands to do things right only for our benefit, with the motivation being selfish in nature. When our chief desire is to see him rise up for himself as a better leader, we are doing it from a right heart. When our heart changes, everything changes.

For the first ten years of our marriage, I wanted to see my husband change the way he was doing this thing or that thing, but mainly for my benefit. The motives behind my prayers at that time were selfish. All the while this caused me to not only build a wall against him, but it also blinded me to my own faults in many ways, and self-righteousness crept in.

It hasn't been until the past six years that my motivation has begun to shift in this area. I really believe the shift began for me as I started to truly pray for my husband—not prayers that were to change him, but prayers that were from a heart of wanting him to be all God has called him to be. I prayed almost daily for several years straight for his inner man. I would pray apostolic prayers (prayers the apostles prayed over the church) over him—prayers for strength, peace, joy, wisdom, etc. What ended up happening was remarkable. My heart began to shift and I saw him differently. My heart expanded as the purity of prayers for his best interests poured from my soul. I began to get a glimpse of what it felt like to desire good for another. I want Antonio, my husband, the other half of me, to be whole, fulfilled, and go to the depths of what is possible with God.

When we pray for our husbands, or anyone for that matter, our heart begins to carry God's heart for that person. Praying for someone, especially when done in secret, is a great display of love, even if they never know about it. No matter the outcome of the situation, this has great worth in the sight of God.

I know that the key to a healthy family, home, and marriage is to have a great leader, and a great leader needs a real support system to get there—not a selfish, self-centered woman who rarely thinks of the benefit of her husband and mainly thinks of her own needs. I know this sounds harsh, but I believe there are many women out there who, like me, lived from a place of selfishness in their heart attitudes toward their spouse.

Even if the things desired are right and good, if they come from a poor motivation, they are tainted. When this type of selfishness is in operation, we are deceived, blinded, and we fail to see the truth about our spouse as God sees it. This is sin and it must be repented of.

Ungratefulness

One of Satan's chief tactics is to create ungratefulness in us toward our spouse. He tempts us to focus on an area of weakness until it is all we see when we look at our spouse. But a grateful heart sees things for what they truly are. When we are grateful, we operate in a principle of God where we can then see the minuteness of what we have focused on in comparison to the rich blessing we have in our husbands. Our husbands are given to us as a gift, and, sadly, many of us squander that gift.

Life is too short to hold resentment and live life trying to benefit only ourselves. The way to live, then, is to give with no conditions, and what better person to give to than the one we love—the man God gave us, our very own gift from God.

Elisabeth Elliot was a woman who was known for reaching the Auca Indians with the Gospel of Jesus Christ after they brutally murdered her missionary husband, Jim. In her book *Let Me Be a Woman*, she tells a story of many women who wrote letters of complaint to a newspaper columnist. They complained over and over again about the countless hours of sleep they lost due to their husbands' snoring. She writes, "Others wrote offering solutions, but the discussion came to an end with one letter, 'Snoring is the sweetest music in the world. Ask any widow.'" She continues:

> How often I have sat in a roomful of people and heard a wife contradict, criticize, belittle, or sneer at her husband before the rest of the company and I have difficulty restraining myself from leaping from my chair, going over to that woman and shaking her by

her shoulders and saying, "Do you realize what you've got?" She doesn't. She hasn't my perspective, of course. If only there was some way for every wife to have the experience of losing her husband for a little time—even of thinking he is dead—in order regain perspective she needs for genuine appreciation.[23]

How sad that we so often do not realize what we have in our husbands. May we never take for granted this incredible lover and friend we have been given.

When we join together in marriage, we are both marrying a sinner, yet we act surprised when sin arises or our expectations are not met. We can choose to focus on the sin or we can pray for, stand with, advocate for, and simply enjoy each other. Elisabeth Elliot concludes, "You may, if you choose, pick away at the 20% (that failed your expectations) for the rest of your married life and probably not reduce it by very much. Or you may skip that and simply enjoy the 80% that is what you hoped for."[24]

Honoring Our Husbands

Peter gives wives good counsel when it comes to honoring our husbands:

> *Wives, in the same way submit yourselves to your own husbands so that, if any of them do not believe the word, they may be won over without words by the behavior of their wives, when they see the purity and reverence of your lives. Your beauty should not come from outward adornment, such as elaborate hairstyles and the wearing of gold jewelry or fine clothes. Rather, it should be that of your inner self, the unfading beauty of a gentle and quiet spirit, which is of great worth in*

God's sight. For this is the way the holy women of the past who put their hope in God used to adorn themselves (1 Peter 3:1-5 NIV).

You may be in a difficult situation in your marriage. You may be praying and believing for breakthrough. The Bible is clear that the way to breakthrough and to winning over your husband is by adorning yourself as the women of old did, through a gentle and quiet spirit. This is not excusing the behavior of a husband who does not do what he is called to do. But his behavior really has no bearing on your obedience. There is something greater here that is at work—God's instituted order of leadership and authority. You may believe that you have an excuse to rebel or take matters into your own hands because your husband is not doing his part, but this is simply not true. In essence, when you are rebelling against your husband, you are rebelling against God. Of course, if your husband is drawing you into sin or asking you to do something that is out of line with God and His Word, you must honor God first. However, it is important to understand that the command of God is not conditional, based upon your husband's actions. We are to submit to God by submitting to our husbands, for when we honor him we honor God.

Tony Evans says much the same thing here:

Instead of doing things God's way and trusting Him for the results...women are using their tongues to dishonor and put down their husbands in the hope that they can break free from what they perceive as the bondage of marriage. But instead of freedom, they find themselves still stranded in a bad situation, because God will never honor rebellion. The Bible says that a wife who honors God creates an opportunity to win her husband over without lecturing, griping, or demeaning him. However, that a husband will eventually come around is a general principle and not guaranteed. The possibility is hard for some wives to believe, because they don't see any way their husbands will ever come around without their intervention.[25]

We cannot say that we are close to God and honoring God while refusing to honor our husband and his leadership. When we honor our husband and operate as a helpmate to him, we ultimately honor God. To respect, honor, and help our husband does not mean we will always agree with him. But it does mean we will trust the leadership of God in our lives as we submit to the model He set out for us.

SPIRITUAL AUTHORITY

A man and his wife living together in harmony form one of the sweetest blessings God has to offer this side of Heaven. Yet it is much more than that. It is a door to a realm of spiritual authority few Christians ever achieve or understand.

God's original purpose in creating humankind is clearly set out in Genesis 1:

> *So God created man in His own image; in the image of God He created him; male and female He created them. Then God blessed them, and God said to them, "Be fruitful and multiply; fill the earth and subdue it; have dominion over the fish of the sea, over the birds of the air, and over every living thing that moves on the earth"* (Genesis 1:27-28).

Commenting on this verse, Derek Prince says, "God did not give dominion of the earth to Adam alone. He was speaking to both Adam and Eve. It was His intention that the man and woman together should rule the earth on His behalf."[26]

One of the main reasons why God made us in His image was to follow His example and operate in leadership. One of the most amazing ways we exercise that leadership is to come into agreement with Him in His command to be fruitful and multiply.

One of the most dynamic ways we exercise our spiritual authority is in creating the unity and harmony we share as a married couple. God's plan for man's dominion on the earth involves not the man on his own, nor the woman on her own, but the man and woman united together in marriage. Just as God is in unity with Himself (Father, Son, and Holy Spirit), His design is for us as His image-bearers to exercise dominion on His behalf as one flesh in the marriage union.

PRAYER OF AGREEMENT

In Matthew 18:18-20, Jesus explains how we can become irresistible in our prayer lives:

> *Assuredly, I say to you, whatever you bind on earth will be bound in heaven, and whatever you loose on earth will be loosed in heaven. Again I say to you that if two of you agree on earth concerning anything that they ask, it will be done for them by My Father in heaven. For where two or three are gathered together in My name, I am there in the midst of them.*

Again, Derek Prince has some helpful advice here:

> The minimum number for agreement in such prayer is two or three. With that basic minimum, whatever that basic minimum, whatever we bind or loose on earth

will be bound or loosed in heaven....This is so exciting because it means that what we say on earth determines what happens in heaven! We may think we are waiting on God to move, which is often true, but there are times when God is waiting for us to move. In a sense that initiative is with us on earth. If we meet the conditions, then whatever we declare on earth is as effective as a decree made in heaven. If we say concerning something on earth, "it is bound," then at that very moment is done in heaven.[27]

This is a true reality, not merely a hope or a wish. It is not magic. The prayer of agreement in marriage is one of the most powerful ingredients for a successful, unified, and dynamic marriage and family. This is where our dominion on the earth truly begins.

The power of the prayer of agreement is one of the main reasons why the enemy strives to stop couples from praying. He understands the power of agreement, and he knows that two hearts joined as one can declare God's Kingdom to be on the earth as it is in Heaven. As a married couple, when we came to understand the magnitude of this truth, it changed our lives and our marriage.

Before 2008, Christelle and I hardly prayed together. We would pray for the food or we would pray about difficult situations, but we would pray separately. We rarely came into agreement in prayer. That all changed when we read a book by Bob and Audrey Meisner called *Marriage Undercover*. It radically changed our marriage and our family.

Praying together brings two hearts together as one. Some would say that it's too difficult for a man to pray with his wife, and others would argue that it's too challenging for a man to spend time reading the Word to his family. This is nonsense. Men, this is a wake-up call to the power of unified prayer with your best friend, your wife. We need leadership in this hour. This is not optional! This is a command from God and a necessity for this hour.

Let me (Antonio) ask you something: If not you, then who? Who will lead your family? Will you allow someone else to lead it? If not now, then when? When will you make the time? When will you make this a priority? According to the Word of God, the husband must lead and set the spiritual direction of the home. There is no better time than the present to begin. God has given you, as the head of the home, the anointing to lead your home, whether you feel qualified or not. There is no greater spiritual leader in your home than you, and the greatest time to start is right now!

We have sought to lay a scriptural foundation for God's greatest blessings in our marriages. When our homes come into right alignment under the authority of Heaven, every blessing from Heaven is released. In fact, the rest of this book is really worthless without this foundation.

If you're a single parent, the rest of this book has many great tools for you. If you are married and you choose to skip over this foundation, your marriage and parenting won't come into alignment with God's plan. We can write more about prayer or the prophetic in the home, and all the other powerful elements of a family encountering God, but if this basic foundation is not laid and cemented, then the rest of the house will simply fall apart.

We encourage you to take time and seek the Lord if there is some part of your home that is not in right alignment with God. We encourage you to repent and ask God for forgiveness. Trust Him, obey Him, and then watch as He begins to set your home on fire!

Chapter 3

THE FIGHT FOR MARRIAGE

For it is in the heart of a man and a woman to share
some sort of quest, to fight some great battle together.
—JOHN AND STASI ELDREDGE, *Love and War**

Recently I (Christelle) had a dream that some very dear friends of ours were getting a divorce. In the dream, a mutual friend called me up on the phone and very casually explained that this couple we both knew was getting a divorce. Apparently, they had difficulty getting along and were ending the marriage because of issues they felt were unresolvable. I was saddened by this news as I thought of their four kids, their life together, and the times we had shared with them.

This mutual friend went on to share in the dream that even she and her husband were struggling, and if something did not change soon they, too, would get a divorce. The shocking thing about the dream was not that these couples were struggling in real life, as I believe every marriage has its struggles, both small and great; rather, it was the offhand, casual way my friends were treating divorce. In my dream, the friend who had called me didn't seem upset by the news she shared; instead, it was almost as if the news justified divorce as the solution for her own marriage problems. She spoke of divorce as if it were just "one of those things," as if she was trying to fix a minor problem like a stalled car or an afternoon headache.

In my dream, I hung up the phone, both heartbroken and stunned. My heart was aching within me and my thoughts were racing. Still dreaming, I went to Antonio and told him what had just happened. He looked at me with great anguish. We cried and prayed for both couples. I remember Antonio kept saying through his sadness, "It's the spirit of divorce; it has turned them against each other." I instinctively knew that all four people in both marriages felt they were right and that they had casually responded by turning on each other with hard hearts. Marriage was not a treasured, valued possession to them; instead, it was simply a status that could be changed at the whim of individual displeasure.

I awoke from this dream deeply saddened and suddenly aware that I myself actually cared more about the harm of divorce in my dream than I did in real life. It was like God was letting me feel His pain over this issue, because the pain I felt in my dream was beyond any pain I had ever felt in my life.

My purpose in sharing this dream is not to downplay hurts and serious issues that arise in many marriages, or to make light of those who have gone through painful divorces. Rather, it is to point out the nonchalant way in which our culture treats marriage. God was showing me that the spirit of divorce is pervading our culture and destroying the family unit of our day.

Currently, in both Christian and non-Christian homes, over 50 percent of all marriages end in divorce. Even in marriages that stay together, the spirit of divorce works overtime to divide and bring disunity between couples as they strive to work through their problems. A marriage is a "union" that is meant to have "unity." Elisabeth Elliot says this about the union of marriage: "There is no competition in a union. There is no playing off of one against the other, no keeping score, no making of comparisons or insistence of fifty-fifty division of anything. Each is for the other, pulling with not against him."[1]

This is the goal of what God intended, and there is great strength in this union. To the degree that a couple can walk in unity, there is power in their marriage. So as we fight for our marriage, greater unity is on the top of the list of what we fight for.

DISPOSABLE MARRIAGES

Relationships today are viewed as disposable. Much of this concept stems from the concept of *disposability* in today's dating culture. It is not uncommon, even in Christian circles, for singles to have multiple boyfriends or girlfriends with no real intent of marrying any one of them. They reason that if it doesn't work out with one person, they will just go on to the next one, and the next one, and the next one, and so the cycle continues. This is perpetuated in our culture through TV shows, movies, and pop songs. Singles today are being taught to *try out* people as if they were used cars. In the meantime, as they are encouraged to be casual and detached, they become emotionally and physically entangled. When we practice this cycle, we are actually "practicing" divorce before we even marry.

Worse still, this *disposable, move-on-to-whomever-makes-me-happy* thinking has been brought into marriage and has trained us to treat our marriages the same way as our dating relationships. This should not be! We are dealing with our brothers and sisters, and someone else's future husband or wife. More importantly, we are dealing with God's son or daughter. We must fight this thinking and become countercultural in the way we live and think in regard to marriage. In fact, we have to kill this type of thinking, or it will kill our marriage.

The truth is that the enemy is scared of the power of the marriage union. He hates marriage for several reasons—the main one being that it is a reflection of the bride (us) and Christ. Great power is released when a couple comes into real unity with each other. One man can chase a thousand (see Josh. 23:10), and two shall put ten thousand to flight (see Deut. 32:29-31). The power of two is completely overwhelming.

Malachi said:

> You cover the altar of the Lord with tears...He does not regard the offering anymore.... Yet you say, "For what reason?" Because the Lord has been witness between you and the wife of your youth, with whom you have dealt treacherously; yet she is your...wife by covenant. ...For the Lord...hates divorce.... Therefore take heed to your spirit, that you do not deal treacherously (Malachi 2:13-14,16).

God hates the sin that causes divorce and its ensuing consequences. Men are leaving "the wife of their youth," divorcing their older wives for much younger women. The Lord calls this "dealing treacherously" with their wives. God hates it when a man or a woman abandons his or her spouse. This passage is not saying that God hates it when His people insist on the biblical grounds for divorce, if absolutely necessary; only that He hates divorce because divorce is division, a separation of what

God called good. No one should be separating what God has put together.

In their book *Love and War,* John and Stasi Eldredge conclude: "When Satan succeeded in deceiving Adam and Eve, the first thing that fractured was their relationship with God; they withdrew from God. The very next fracture was in their marriage; they withdrew from one another. Certainly this was his intent all along. Divide and conquer."[2]

The number of people we know who have divorced or are getting divorced saddens us. We feel pain each time we hear of a family that is torn apart and has to suffer through the agony of a broken union. One thing we desire is to be a caretaker of the heart of God. God hates divorce, and, as followers of Christ, we must *fight* to hate what God hates and love what He loves.

When we speak of such a sensitive issue, we are not taking this lightly or minimizing the pain that a person may have suffered. Our heart is to see couples restored, living in intimacy and fighting for their marriage, even in the most difficult of times. Once we see the scope of the assault the enemy has undertaken on our homes and marriages, we can begin to be filled with a righteous anger that says, "No more casualties!" But it must begin in our own home first.

CASUALNESS LEADS TO CASUALTIES

I think we can all agree that it is a fierce battle to not only preserve our marriages, but to build marriages that thrive. The question needs to be asked: If this is a battle we are fighting, why do we treat it with such a casual attitude? One thing that I (Antonio) like to watch are war documentaries. I have seen many of these films, and I am always intrigued by how these wars are fought, what factors influenced the wins and losses, and what strategies the leaders implemented under battle conditions. Honestly, everything about war interests me.

Soldiers take war very seriously. They train hard, they endure grueling conditions, they go without many basic comforts, and they even give their lives all for one thing—*victory*. We can all agree that marriage is a battleground that *we must fight to win*. If we engage in a real war with a casual attitude, it will result in only one thing—casualties. In the war on marriage, those casualties will be married couples and their children.

We would never dream of simply strolling nonchalantly through a World War II battlefield where bullets are whizzing past our heads, bombs and mines are exploding all around us, all the while hoping to not only survive, but win the battle. No! We would train, create and study a battle plan, study the enemy's tactics, and, most importantly, be alert and ready! Therefore, it is our desire to give you some battle plans so that you can not only *defend* your marriage but also go on the *offensive*. So here we go.

Stop Saying "Divorce"

For starters, refuse to say the word *divorce*. Most couples get married with hopes of success, setting out with a dream of a life filled with love, unity, happiness, and fulfillment. I don't know about you, but that's how we started our marriage. We believe that no matter what you have been through, you can have the kind of marriage you dreamed about, because with God all things are possible (see Matt. 19:26).

One roadblock we have seen to having the marriage of your dreams is a simple thought that can be tucked away quietly in the back of your mind. This thought is about a way of escape if things get bad—*divorce*. We know that nobody sets out wanting a divorce or even thinking they will be a casualty of it. In reality, we leave this escape hatch "open" when we operate in the spirit of divorce by sleeping on the couch after a fight, or by hurling the word "divorce" at each other when we are angry. One of the best decisions to make as a married couple is to agree to never even *say* the word *divorce* or operate in the spirit of it in any way.

We realize there are situations of adultery, abandonment, and even danger that must be considered on an individual basis. But even in the case of adultery, if the offender is repentant and wants the marriage to succeed, reconciliation can lead to a great blossoming of a wonderful life together. This was the case for our friends Bob and Audrey Meisner. They have written many books and have given their lives to fighting for families. With God, anyone can have a better marriage than they ever hoped or dreamed for, no matter the circumstances!

Every couple who wants to can have a dream marriage, one that is ten out of ten. We believe God can restore and heal every situation, no matter how broken. We have not only seen it in our own marriage but in many others as well. God specializes in healing, and when He heals He makes the covenant better than before—if we let go and let Him. When we lean on the Lord, He breaks in with His grace and power, restores our souls, heals our wounds, and makes all things new if we dare to believe Him for it.

BUILDING THE FOUNDATION

There is so much to be said about marriage, and we cannot even begin to lay out in this book all there is in building a great marriage. What we do hope to do, however, is inspire you to study what it means to be a godly husband or wife so that you can do your part in building a powerful marriage union. Whether you have been married for many years or you are just starting out in training for the battle, we hope to give you the tools for success.

We have had many young couples ask us what would be our best advice for them as they are starting out in marriage. Here is our advice summed up in one paragraph: Pray together, be best friends, love God and each other with all your heart, laugh together, make love lots, repent quickly, and forgive even quicker. As a couple, commit to keeping short accounts, live transparently, pursue each other, and, most importantly, pursue God with everything in you. Doing these things is not always easy; in fact, rarely is it easy, but it is worth it. Just one of the things in this list is a book in itself and the pursuit of it is a lifelong journey.

When we pursue God, we get closer to each other. It is like a triangle with God at the top and one spouse at each corner. When we get nearer to God, our nearness to each other increases. Nothing of value comes without cost, but the cost of a good marriage is nothing compared to the rich rewards we will enjoy. When we build a *good* foundation in marriage, we build a *great* foundation for our children and the generations that follow. It is worth fighting for!

PRAYING TOGETHER

A great key to making our marriage succeed has been prayer. There is no better way to fight for your marriage than by praying together regularly. In a season of hardship in our own marriage, we picked up a book called *Marriage Undercover.* In this book, Bob and Audrey share their incredible story of heartache, redemption, and forgiveness as they walked through the pain of infidelity and experienced God's healing power. We learned much from them, and, as we neared the end of their book, we came across a method they recommended when praying together as a couple. They wrote:

> Prayer is one of the most powerful weapons for covering that we have in our spiritual arsenal. In America, the divorce rate is approximately one out of every two couples, even among couples who attend church regularly. According to a Gallup poll, for Christian couples who pray together daily, the divorce rate drops to one out of every 1,152! Leo told us that out of 10,000 couples he had counseled, he had never met a couple that prayed together daily that had gotten a divorce.[3]

This is a statistic not to be ignored, and it gives us even more motivation to have a life of prayer. We wanted to have a marriage that beat the statistics, and this new method of prayer caught our eye. At this time of our life we had just rededicated our lives, home, and marriage back to the Lord, and this method became something that led our house to become a house of prayer. Let us share it with you straight from their book:

> Essentially it is a very simple prayer model (and simple is usually the best kind). Begin by looking at each other face to face and eye to eye. Try to find Jesus in each other. Remember, *He* is your source, your answer, and your supreme love. As you pray, focus on three things:
>
> **Thankfulness**. Take turns expressing what you are thankful for that day, not just in general but also what you are thankful for about each other.
>
> **Repentance**. Once again, take turns asking if there is anything that either of you hurt the other with today. If

so, before God and your spouse, confess it and repent of it. The only response the other should make is, "I forgive you."

Bless each other. Speak blessing and goodness to each other. This will help each of your focus on the positives about each other rather than the negatives.[4]

If you do not pray together regularly, I challenge you to begin doing this. It is an easy way to start, and it really only takes 10–15 minutes a day. If it happens to you as it did for us, you will begin to enjoy a newfound intimacy and power—your prayer times will become longer and longer, simply because you will love it.

PURPOSE OF BEING TOGETHER

There are several reasons for the purpose of the marriage union. One important aspect is that of *dominion*. God placed Adam and Eve in the Garden of Eden and gave them some instructions: *"Then God blessed them, and God said to them, 'Be fruitful and multiply; fill the earth and subdue it; have dominion over the fish of the sea, over the birds of the air, and over every living thing that moves on the earth'"* (Gen. 1:28).

The picture that is given here is one of rulership, extending, and governing. In Genesis, God confided to man that he could not do these things alone—he needed help. So God created the best person possible to help man—*a woman*.

Adam was lord over the Garden and was God's representative in the Garden. He was the keeper of the Garden, and he was the protector of it. Man and woman were both there to rule and govern together, but one was the leader and protector of it and the other one was the helper in doing it.

Andreas J. Kostenberger and David W. Jones, in their book *God, Marriage, and Family*, write, "Genesis 2 does not teach that she may merely act as the man's 'helper' when she so chooses but rather that serving as the man's 'helper' sums up her very reason for existence in relation to the man."[5]

FRIENDSHIP IN MARRIAGE

Another key purpose for marriage is friendship. "It is not a lack of love," said Friedrich Nietzsche, "but a lack of friendship that makes unhappy marriages."[6] The Bible goes on to describe:

> *God put the Man into a deep sleep. As he slept He removed one of his ribs and replaced it with flesh. God then used the rib that He had taken from the Man to make Woman and presented her to the Man. The Man said, "Finally! Bone of my bone, flesh of my flesh! Name her Woman for she was made from Man." Therefore a man leaves his father and mother and embraces his wife. They become one flesh. The two of them, the Man and his Wife, were naked, but they felt no shame* (Genesis 2:21-25 MSG).

God saw a great need in Adam right from the beginning. Adam had God, animals, a beautiful untainted earth, yet God saw him and said he needed a companion, a friend. Whether Adam knew it or not, he needed a real friend, a loyal companion, a human partner who looked like him and yet was the complete opposite of him, who fit him like a puzzle, and who was *of him* yet different *from him*.

This is a great mystery, the mystery of marriage. God designed woman and fashioned her, yet man himself was the *clay* that He used to do so. God did this for man as a gift to him. Man could not lead alone. She was made from his very body. This explains why he desired to protect her, love her, and cover her—it was really like protecting himself. This is why Scripture reminds men to love their wives as their own bodies—he was meant to live this way.

STORIES OF LEADERS WHO FAILED IN FRIENDSHIP

Without friendship in marriage, we will live a lonely life. Marriage is two imperfect people walking face to face by the grace of God. What happens when we have two people who love Jesus but walk imperfectly toward each other? What happens when one or both spouses give themselves to spending time caring for the children more than each other? What happens when we invest our time in our work instead of in our wife and family? What happens when a man doesn't take care of his spouse because he becomes so blinded by success or the call of God that he misses his greatest call in loving his spouse? You get loneliness and regret.

A book from Focus on the Family titled *The Best Advice I Ever Got on Marriage* states, "You'll find countless volumes on romance, intimacy, and passion in marriage, but not much on the simple act of being good friends as husband and wife. It seems friendship is secondary to romance in the minds of many. Gallup's research indicates that a couple's friendship quality could account for 70 percent of overall marital satisfaction."[7]

Let us give you some examples of how important friendship is by looking at the lives of great leaders in church history. We have learned a multitude of wonderful things on what various revivalists, reformers, and preachers of the Gospel did for the Kingdom of God—a simple study into any one of their lives will illustrate how they forever changed the world for Christ. In many ways, it seems as though their lives were inexplicably perfect.

However, after probing deeper, we were saddened by what we found. Although we have great respect for these leaders, we have learned some valuable lessons from them of what *not to do* in marriage. Our intent is not to taint their credibility as preachers of the Gospel; our desire is to shed light on the mistakes of their home life so as not to repeat them. We hope that these stories bring wisdom and strength to your own life, and that you learn from them as we did.

John Wesley

Everyone knows John Wesley (1703–1791) as the father of the Methodist movement. He was a powerful preacher, mobilizer, and trainer. He changed the face of Christianity in so many ways that we still continue to feel the effects of his ministry today. However, John chose to make his ministry call more important than his call to be a husband. Referencing the journals of Wesley, Doreen Moore elaborates:

> When John Wesley married Molly Vazeille he determined he would not "preach one sermon or travel one day less in a married than in a single state." Initially his wife travelled with him, but the hardships were difficult and she stopped. After that she rarely saw him. Although he wanted to accommodate her desires, he stopped short of anything that would interfere with the cause of Christ. He believed that if he slackened at all, even for her, he would be disobedient to the work God had called him to. To this cause John Wesley desired to "spend to be spent." Their relationship deteriorated and she often left him. In 1771, he wrote, "I have not

left her; I have not sent her away; I will not recall her."
John Wesley believed "the cause of Christ" took precedence over family.[8]

Their marriage was a sad one, and they finished their lives on earth distant and estranged from each other. Although John loved Jesus, he did not see God's heart for marriage. He ministered to everyone but his own wife.

A.W. Tozer

Aiden Wilson Tozer (1897–1963) was one of the greatest pastors, preachers, and writers in the twentieth century. He wrote many books that have impacted a lot of people, including us, with their sound biblical truths. Aiden was a man of deep faith and unprecedented devotion to Christ. He spent long hours in study, meditation on the Word, and time in worship to God. Sadly, his life was one of drastic contrasts. He had the ability to captivate even the most trained theologians, yet he neglected his basic responsibilities as a husband and a father. While his life is inspirational, it holds a solemn warning for all of us.

Two key areas in A.W. Tozer's life held him back. In an attempt to protect his heart and his family from worldliness, he maintained a theology of poverty. As a result, he didn't take his full salary as a pastor and he relinquished his book royalties and speaking honorariums. Even though he became a household name in the Christian world, he never owned a car. He, his wife, Ada, and their seven children walked everywhere, even during the punishing Chicago winters. At times the family would take the bus or ask for rides from friends. When he died, he left his wife with no savings at all.

Aiden and Ada lived very lonely lives and had a marriage that was marked with detachment and disappointment. He devoted his life to extensive prayer, preaching, writing, traveling, and mentoring others. This left him with no time to develop the marital intimacy that they had both learned to live without. To his parishioners, they appeared to be a happily married couple. And, on one level, they were. After decades of faithfully walking together in their separate worlds of existence, they had found a relatively comfortable level of accommodation.

Before he died in 1963, A.W. Tozer encouraged Ada to reach out to another man named Leonard Odam, who was a widower. Ada married Leonard one year after Aiden's death and lived happily married for ten years. Leonard taught her how to drive a car, and she felt connected to her husband. Her response to several friends who asked her how she was doing was consistent: "I have never been happier in my life. Aiden loved Jesus Christ, but Leonard Odam loves me."[9]

A.W. Tozer made the grave mistake of going into the mission field while neglecting the mission field of his own home.

John G. Lake

Another great leader whom we have learned and gleaned from over the years is John G. Lake (1870–1935). Lake was from Canada and was a sacrificial missionary, preacher, and healing evangelist. He saw some of the greatest workings of God where thousands of people were miraculously healed in his meetings. He was a man used powerfully by God, yet he also made the same grave mistake of sacrificing his family on the altar of his ministry.

John G. Lake was married twice. He married his first wife, Jennie, in 1893. They loved each other, and she was perfect for him. In 1908, he, Jennie, and their seven children moved to Africa to become missionaries. They immediately had a thriving ministry where countless people were giving their lives to Christ and were being physically healed. People would travel to John's home if they could not attend the meetings he held, and oftentimes the crowd was so large that Jennie did not have time to prepare meals for the family.[10]

Lake would never receive offerings at his services, but he would often find food and money left anonymously on the family's doorstep. As the husband and father, it was John's responsibility to bring home groceries for the large family; however, if John met someone in need along the way home (for example, a widow who had hungry children) he would give everything he had to the one in need. Food always seemed to be in short supply. These ministry habits of her husband were difficult for Jennie to adapt to while they ministered in Africa.[11]

Roberts Liardon writes of Lake, "On December 22, 1908, Jennie died. John was stunned. Most accounts of Jennie Lake's death attribute it to malnutrition and physical exhaustion. When John was away, scores of sick people would wait on his lawn until he returned. So Jennie would feed them while they waited with what little food she could spare."[12] The price for sacrificing the people you love the most is high. Our jobs and callings are never more important than the call to our families.

Many times the children had resentment and bitterness toward their fathers. Liardon went on to say, "Lake's children from his first marriage to Jennie suffered greatly because of his absence. Even when he was present in the room, he would drift away in meditation, being constantly mindful of the ministry and the Lord. Because of this, the children often felt neglected. Each of his children developed very hardened attitudes toward their father. Their lives were characterized by bitterness. Lake grieved over his lack of attention given the children. And he would later write in a letter that the many miracles wrought at his hands were personally unfulfilling and not worth the loss of his family."[13]

Even though John G. Lake made tragic mistakes with his first wife and family, he made things right with his second marriage and family. He later married Florence, and "found the key to being a good husband, involved father, and powerful minister. His children had a different attitude toward him. They remembered him as a man who loved to laugh and enjoy his friends."[14]

The reason we shared these stories was so that we can learn from the mistakes and failures of these great men, so that we don't have to repeat them. If we have these tendencies or have made these mistakes, we must look at them and change them. There is great hope through repentance, forgiveness, and the grace of God. We believe in hope—God's hope.

We believe that a marriage is strong when there is a strong friendship at its foundation. Loving unconditionally, considering each other, serving one another, and laying our lives down for each other is founded on the wellspring of a deep and intimate friendship. Without this, we have a relationship of forced obligations, where we reluctantly put up with each other so that we are little more than just roommates. This is a lonely life.

Jonathan Edwards

We wanted to leave the story of Jonathan and Sarah Edwards for the end, to inspire you with an incredible example of a real, amazing marriage and the fruit of their marriage, the Edwards children. Regardless of where you find yourself today, take hope in the story of the marriage and family of Jonathan and Sarah Edwards.

John Maxwell, in his book *Today Matters*, writes of Jonathan Edwards, "He was a theologian, pastor, and president of Princeton. He was born in 1703 and lived in Connecticut, New York, Massachusetts, and New Jersey. He and his wife Sarah had eleven children—three sons and eight daughters. They remained married for thirty-one years until he died of fever following a small pox inoculation."[15]

Jonathan and Sarah had a great marriage that was distinguished by love, respect, friendship, and intimacy. Though Jonathan would often be in his study upwards of 13 hours a day, Sarah would spend many of these hours with him. They would pray together at least once a day, discuss religion together, and have devotions together at night when the rest of the family had gone to bed. Sarah's happiness was something that Jonathan was strongly committed to. He said in one of his sermons that husbands and wives were to "study to render each other's lives comfortable."[16]

As a Christian father, Edwards was faithful, tender, and affectionate toward his children when they were born. He was committed to them as he was to Sarah, and he would daily spend time with his family relaxing and enjoying each other's company.[17]

Jonathan and Sarah had an incredible friendship. George Mardsen, in *A Life of Jonathan Edwards*, writes that while Edwards was on his deathbed, he said these words to his daughter Lucy about his wife: "Give my kindest love to my dear wife, and tell her, that the uncommon union, which has so long subsisted between us, has been of such a nature, as I trust is spiritual and therefore will continue forever."[18]

Mardsen then tells us of Sarah's profound response to her daughter when she heard of her husband's death: "The Lord has done it. He has made me adore His goodness, that we had him so long. But my God lives; and he has my heart. O what a legacy my husband and your father has left us! We are all given to God and there I am and love to be."[19]

History shows that Jonathan and Sarah left a legacy that has impacted the nations. By the year 1900, their descendants "included 13 college presidents, 65 professors, 100 lawyers and a dean of a law school, 30 judges, 66 physicians and a dean of a medical school, and 80 holders of public office, including three US Senators, mayors of three large cities, governors of three states, a Vice-President of the United States, and a controller of the United States Treasury."[20] They had written over 100 books and edited journals and periodicals. Many were missionaries while others served on mission boards. Others directed banks, banking houses, and insurance companies, and had owned or been superintendents of large coal mines, silver mines, and iron plants. This is a supreme example of the impact an on-fire marriage and family can have on nations and generations. Take heart!

CONFLICT

As we have learned from these great leaders, conflict and differences come into every marriage. It's impossible not to have them, because we are selfish by nature. Every person is born self-centered. This basic fact of human nature is only encouraged by the messages we get from media to serve our own needs and make ourselves happy. As a result, when we're not happy in marriage we just leave. We must have "fallen out of love," or had "irreconcilable differences." Gary Thomas says, "Marriages don't necessarily choose to grow apart but they stop fighting and choosing to stay together. It's the second law of thermodynamics, that things are naturally pulling apart, things are naturally going into ruin. It is so easy for this to happen in a marriage through parenting, vocation, your own avocations and hobbies."[21]

Again, he continues and says, "Much of our marital dissatisfaction actually stems from self-hatred. We don't like what we've done or become; we've let selfish and sinful attitudes poison our thoughts and lead us into shameful behaviors, and suddenly all we want is out. The mature response, however, is not to leave, it's to change—ourselves."[22]

The key to the fastest resolutions in marriage is not justifying our selfishness. From the time we are babies and through our growing-up years, we are self-centered and self-satisfying. We think about what will make us happy. As we mature in God, our goal must change. We must choose to kill our selfishness and become generous givers and considerate servants. This service is not circumstantial or in response to someone else's good deeds, but even despite them. Acts 20:35 says, *"It is more blessed to give than to receive."* This is how a friendship grows and matures. This is what makes a marriage strong, enduring the test of time and becoming a testimony for generations to come.

I love the question Gary Thomas poses in *Sacred Marriage*: "What if God designed marriage to make us holy more than make us happy?"[23] We get so many false ideas of marriage from the books and movies we feed ourselves with. Marriage is established and sustained by an unselfish attitude, that of giving to each other until death do us part.

Marriage will make us happy as we give of ourselves to our spouse. Gary Thomas again says:

> There have been numerous longitudinal studies of marriage that have charted out what you see in the average

marriage. There are certain seasons when you would expect a marriage to take a real hit in the sense of intimacy and satisfaction. Couples tend to marry on a high point or rather get together on a high point. There is often a real wake-up call in that first year where some couples start to panic. And then when you bring kids into the house, it usually takes another huge dip. When you have toddlers and babies, you can't expect the satisfaction to be the same because you're just exhausted. It's hard to keep that time together. You're just pulled in all of these directions. However, studies have also shown that if that couple will stay together they will experience that same satisfaction as when they first got together. But it's even a deeper meaning. Their brains have formed around each other; you have memories of raising a family together. You're comfortable in each other's presence.[24]

A marriage relationship is difficult even at its best, and it is a daily choice. You can choose to ignore it and grow cold toward each other, or you can choose to develop it and see positive growth. The problems within marriage can be addressed and fixed if you work at rebuilding. Whether your marriage does not hold the place of priority it should, you stopped praying together, have lost spiritual intimacy, or you have stopped enjoying each other as you did at first, you can choose to work at rebuilding.[25]

INTIMACY WAS THE BEGINNING INTENT

The intimacy that was intended by God is apparent right from the beginning of creation. Adam and Eve were "naked and felt no shame." Their nakedness was not just physical nakedness, but a nakedness of heart and emotion, a transparent, soul-baring friendship that could only culminate in physical intimacy. Adam and Eve experienced together the kind of *nakedness* that you know when you are with yourself, for they were *of* each other. Likewise, we are meant to care for each other like we care for our own selves, for we are made of the same substance.

God intended our marriages to be a beautiful picture of Jesus Christ and His church. He desires for us to walk out a life of wholeness as one together in marriage, displaying Christ to the world. Paul said that marriage is a great mystery (see Eph. 5:32), which perhaps explains why we sometimes have such a hard time understanding it. Marriage is better experienced than understood.

FIGHTING FOR EACH OTHER

Too often in marriage, we have resorted to fighting for our own agendas instead of fighting for each other. More importantly, we have neglected to fight for God's original intent. Today, the phrase *fighting for marriage* has come to mean fighting against same-sex unions or solving a marital crisis. Although these are good and worthwhile efforts, fighting for marriage should mean to fight for the vision of Genesis 2, the model of marriage that Adam and Eve experienced before the fall and that reflects our future marriage with our Bridegroom God, Jesus Christ.

Adam looked at Eve and exclaimed, "At last! Bone of by bone, flesh of my flesh"; in other words, he saw in Eve *the part of him that was missing*. We want to raise the standard that God originally set out for us, where we love each other as we love ourselves, because we are *of* each other. Let's use our marriage as the powerful weapon in our hand that it is and crush the enemy with it.

No matter where you find your marriage today, whether you are experiencing heartache, betrayal, coldness, or distance, begin to fight again. Start by praying for your spouse, but pray like you would pray for *yourself.* Change your perspective to God's perspective today. Fight for unity, intimacy, respect, and love. Get into unity wherever you can and go after more of it each day. Fight *for* your spouse, not *against* them. Be on his or her team, because it is actually your team. Ask God for revelation of what He intended in marriage from the time of Adam until now.

Also, begin to meditate on what it means to have a marriage that looks like Christ and His church. Ask God to show you where you have not walked in this original intent, begin to change it, and repent to your spouse. See your spouse as the answer to the need in your heart for earthly companionship and intimacy. Rebuild bridges, repent, forgive, restore, love unconditionally, long for your spouse like Jesus longs for us, don't be afraid of getting hurt, and out-give each other! When you begin to see things God's way, you will see so much bigger than yourself; you will see the great power that your own marriage carries.

LOVING GOD LEADS TO LOVING EACH OTHER

The psalmist declared:

One thing I have desired of the Lord, that will I seek: that I may dwell in the house of the Lord all the days of my life, to behold the beauty of the Lord, and to inquire in His temple (Psalm 27:4).

In life we seek many things, but we must let our longing for God be our chief desire. David's cry was his declaration to God for his life, "There is only one thing I want! I want You, to look at

You, to see Your beauty, to inquire of You; I want You, God, above all else!" Imagine his principal aspiration in life being this one thing. He was a king, a general, a husband, and a father. He had all the accolades, praises, and endless responsibilities that his life demanded. Yet he cried out for God with all his entire being: "I just want You!"

When our number one cry is to know God and to see Him, then He becomes our life's preoccupation. When this happens we begin to understand His heart, His desires, and His longings to the point where we begin to reflect His image. In our own marriage, the more we pursue God, the more our hearts grow for each other. Making God your one desire is the greatest gift you can give your spouse. It will transform your home. You cannot have a truly tender heart toward God and not begin to be transformed into a person who loves better.

When we pursue God, we are pursuing His ways. His ways are ways of love, tenderness, and a desire for us to have a great marriage full of life and longing for one another. When we love God first, we will love our spouse. Ask God, "What do You think about my husband/wife? What do You think about my marriage?" He will tell you, and you will see your spouse with His eyes and His heart. But you must have Him be your one desire, the One you seek after with all your being. And part of seeking after Him is to pursue your spouse, for that is His desire for you. He knows that you will have great fulfillment in this age through that partner—your gift for life. You will also have a foretaste of what is to come.

When we get married, we long for intimacy, friendship, and partnership; someone we can be free to be ourselves with; someone to love and who loves us in return. God designed us this way. Marriage is a glimpse, a shadow, of that consummation we will have at the glorious wedding supper of the Lamb. We will be joined forever to the One we are really longing for. You only have one life to be married to your spouse—so enjoy your marriage with everything that is in you. Live with no regrets, for this is God's desire for you!

Chapter 4

PRUNING THAT LEADS TO INTIMACY

The fruitfulness of tomorrow is contingent upon today.
—Antonio and Christelle Baldovinos

Have you ever heard the expression, "Be careful what you wish for"? Though we didn't realize it until months later, what we began to experience entering 2012 was exactly what we had prayed for. We turned the page on a new year, and shortly thereafter we found ourselves in one of the hardest and most challenging times of our marriage, not realizing all along that it was what we had been praying for.

As a couple, as a family, and as a ministry, we were praying to experience the full extent of all that God had for our lives, the fullness that God has for us on this side of Heaven. We didn't want to live our lives looking back with regret or missed opportunities. In our short marriage we already had regrets, so from that point onward we resolved to live each day free of regret. A life worth living is best done fully abandoned and without regrets.

In the course of life, we overestimate the future, exaggerate the past, and undervalue the process of today—the present. What happens today is our springboard for tomorrow, and our yesterday is what we're able to take into today. Today is the most significant time that we have. Taking hold of all that God has for us, our marriage, and our family is one of the most important resolves that we can make on this journey of life.

PRUNING THAT PRODUCES FRUIT (CHRISTELLE)

In the middle of January 2012, Antonio and I had several reoccurring words and themes that came to the forefront of our attention. I first had a dream where there were several things shown to me that were stealing from and distracting us as a family from going deeper with God. At this time, we were contending in prayer for revival to come in any form that God would send. He was beginning to highlight things that were in the way of us taking hold of the fullness that He had in store.

During this time, I was drawn to John 15 and was meditating on abiding in Him and Him in me. I felt that God was highlighting that He wanted to take us through a season of pruning. I told this to Antonio without really knowing what it meant or would entail. Even at that point we began to reignite the fire within us and remove from our lives areas that were producing dullness and hindering us.

I found myself studying John 15 for several weeks, trying to take in that chapter and its richness. One week after this, I tuned in to the IHOP-KC weekend service to find Allen Hood (one of my favorite teachers) preaching a sermon called "Responding Well During a Season of Pruning." Though I could not believe that was what Allen was talking about, it confirmed in my heart that God was going to take us into a season of pruning. I knew that how I responded mattered just as much as the pruning itself.

GOING INTO A PRUNING SEASON (ANTONIO)

On the same day that Christelle was hearing the teaching from Allen Hood, I had a young man who attends our prayer meetings (and various other ministry events) nervously say a prophetic word to me that he sensed was from God. He said to me, "You're going to be going through a season of pruning." He went on to say, "That may sound bad, but the promise from God is that because of the pruning, you will bear much fruit."

I went home after receiving that word, knowing in my heart that we would be going through a pruning season, but not knowing what that really meant. Christelle and I spoke about what took place during the day. Initially I thought it would be about pruning some area or person within our ministry. The last thing I thought about was going through a season of pruning personally, or even within our marriage. I also thought that it wasn't that big of a deal—pruning was almost like taking tweezers and going through a bonsai tree. It was kind of like needing a haircut. However, going through a season of pruning is different; God had much more in store for us.

WHAT DOES PRUNING REALLY MEAN?

I am the true vine, and My Father is the vinedresser. Every branch in Me that does not bear fruit He takes away; and every branch that bears fruit He prunes, that it may bear more fruit (John 15:1-2).

In the natural, pruning of trees is very important. A horticultural specialist states that the "primary objective of...pruning is to develop a strong tree framework that will support fruit production. Improperly trained fruit trees generally have very upright branch angles, which result in serious limb breakage under a heavy fruit load. This significantly reduces the productivity of the tree and may greatly reduce tree life."[1]

Pruning is important and necessary so that we can carry heavier loads of fruitfulness in our lives; without it, limbs can be broken. It minimizes disease and brings strength for the long term. It helps trees resist failure, provides freedom for branches to grow, and promotes longer life. If we really want fruitfulness and long-term endurance in our marriages and families, seasons of pruning are inevitable—in fact, they are necessary.

While going through a pruning season (which I believe every person, marriage, home, and even businesses and ministries will experience), one has to have the end in mind. Knowing that God disciplines those He loves is imperative. Realizing that a pruning season will allow for fruitfulness to come forth is also very important. And another vital element is that a pruning season comes to a fruitful believer or marriage, giving the hope of greater fruitfulness in the next season.

Entering into a season of pruning should always be welcomed if viewed correctly. Going through a pruning season is challenging, hard, and even painful, but the fruit that can come out is truly glorious. It is one of the ways God brings forth fruit in our lives. Everything that lasts will come from fierce struggle.

Allen Hood says, "In pruning, the Word that was cultivated from the previous season is tested for its genuineness, and the present trial forces us to internalize new realities from the Word which will yield fruitfulness only in the next season."[2] In other words, the fruitfulness of tomorrow is contingent upon today. Hood goes on to say, "A season of pruning can bring a loss of finances, possessions, impact, influence, position, stature, relationship, and opportunity. To be pruned is to lose the basis upon which everyone around you measures you as successful."[3]

Adversity, testing, and pruning are the processes for success or the next season of fruitfulness. Most people would rather go along the road mostly traveled. They believe this road will include comfort, coasting, and living the status quo, which additionally includes no testing at all. But a successful marriage goes through testing and perseveres. Failure in anything is simply to quit in the face of adversity. How we deal with pruning, and look beyond it, impacts every aspect of our life, both for today and tomorrow.

As humans, we run away from adversity and challenges; we run away from testing and sprint to comfort as fast as possible. When we are hungry, we get food. When we are thirsty, we run for a drink. When we are tired, we run to rest. When we are weak, we run to find strength. Our natural psyche is to run to green pastures and prevent any kind of desert time. We aren't saying this tendency is entirely bad; however, we don't naturally have a positive outlook when adversity enters our lives. If we want growth, strength, and fruitfulness for years to come, we must go through testing, adversity, pruning, and challenges. James 1 and Romans 5 both exhort us to consider and welcome testing with joy, and to embrace it because it ultimately produces character.

LIVING A FACE-TO-FACE MARRIAGE

This wasn't the only time that our marriage was tested; however, we were better prepared because we had grown from the previous season of adversity and challenges. Every challenge we faced in our marriage was quite different, and every time it exposed our heart in a new light.

Since 2008, God did a great work in our marriage, restoring us. It was a night-and-day difference. In July of 2008, while on a long trip driving through the northern part of the U.S., en route to see family in the Midwest, we felt led to write down some dreams that we had for our future. One of these dreams was to live a *face-to-face* life with each other. We didn't know how we would get there, but we knew we wanted it. Since that time, we have continually spoken of the marriage that we started out our life dreaming about.

From the day a couple gets married, they all have some form of expectations of what their marriage will be like. Some expectations are good, but most are fairy tales. Many women have an expectation of their "Prince Charming," and that their husband will understand their feelings at every moment of every day. Many times a woman will have expectations of their husband listening to them for hours, enjoying the things they enjoy, caring for their emotions, and being their support. They expect to be romanced regularly, while the man is learning their tastes and being full of surprises. This is followed by long conversations in the evenings and never fighting. They also have expectations of their husband caring for their physical needs, being their spiritual leaders, and putting them first before anything else.

On the other hand, men have expectations of what they think is the perfect woman. They may expect their wife to cook food, as well as clean and have the house spotless. They may have expectations to work alongside them, and, in today's culture, bring in an income at the same time. They also may think that their woman will always be sexy, will walk around naked in their bedroom and give them endless sex. A man may expect his wife to be barefoot and pregnant in the kitchen, while at the same time looking like Barbie. He may expect her to submit, never disagree, and follow his lead in all situations, while she may only take the helm when he doesn't want to—especially in spiritual needs.

Some of these expectations are a fairy-tale fantasy because of what we have seen in movies or have read in some magazine, and some of these are outright sinful. These expectations for men and women are not reality. Secretly, some may even have the mindset that if their needs and expectations are met, then they will respond accordingly to meet the other's expectations as well. Marriage has become circumstantial, with a deserving and fair-based mindset, instead of being filled with unconditional love and respect. It has become self-serving instead of self-giving.

One expectation and desire that we should have (which is God-given) is to live our married lives face to face. In Genesis, Adam and Eve were in the Garden, where *"they were both naked, the man and his wife, and were not ashamed"* (Gen. 2:25). This is living face to face in every way as a married couple. God placed this transparent, vulnerable, trusting need to be fulfilled within relationship. There is an inherent desire that we will be accepted and unconditionally loved—no matter what. Adam and Eve lived face to face spiritually, physically, and emotionally; this is meant to be in marriage, and it is a natural God-given longing.

WHERE THE PRUNING STARTED (ANTONIO)

Our ministry runs a five-month discipleship school called the Pursuit Internship. The first three months is the lecture phase, where we have biblical, experiential teaching on a variety of subjects. Following these three months, most of the staff and students go to a developing nation where they preach the Gospel, teach, and take what they have learned into ministry outreach.

During the first three months, we bring in first-class teachers on specific subjects. Sometimes I would be the person to pick these speakers up from the airport. I picked up one speaker and asked what was going on in his life and ministry. For some reason, he started speaking to me about the various challenges their ministry was going through, with sexual immorality in their midst, inappropriate dress, and many other things. We spoke for hours about these issues. I had a growing burden for greater purity in my own life and ministry. I had also seen questionable things in our ministry, with our own staff. However, because these were more suspicions than actual facts, I dismissed them.

I had also felt that I needed to share struggles and secrets that I had pertaining to lust and sexual immorality with Christelle, as well as past sins that I had kept a secret from her. For quite some time God had been highlighting this to me. This would have been very difficult, and even hurtful, which is the main reason why I didn't want to share them with her in the first place.

During the week, the speaker stayed at our home and had a dream one night. That morning I walked from my bedroom and he was sitting in my living room waiting for me. He said he had some strong words for me and that God had spoken to him about me. He also said, "You have some things to deal with, and you know what I'm talking about."

After ruminating on some of these thoughts and feelings all week long, I felt conviction mount up to share all hidden things with Christelle, but I was still reserved and not fully convinced I should. I knew God not only wanted to deal with the past by confessing past sins, but He also wanted to protect our future with regular communication about the hard stuff.

It Begins with Confession

As I dropped the speaker off at the airport, it worked out that the next week's speaker was arriving one hour later. Unbeknownst to me, where my conversation ended with the last speaker, it continued with the next week's speaker. None of it was set up by me, but I knew this was the pruning season God was talking about months prior. I had forgotten about it, but I now knew this was where God wanted to take us.

As soon as I dropped off the speaker for the week, I asked to speak with Christelle. We went into a private time, where we would be alone with no interruptions, and I struggled sharing some of the hardest things that she would ever hear. Some of it was over ten years old. She in turn shared things with me that were hard for me to hear. Neither of us were prepared to hear these things, and in reality we didn't know how to handle them in the days, weeks, and months following. We needed God, and we both wanted transparency, with no hiddenness and no shame. This was the beginning of that face-to-face marriage we dreamed about years prior.

God not only wanted to show us how to communicate easy stuff, but the hard stuff as well. He was teaching us how to confess to each other in marriage; He was teaching us how to forgive, deal with hurt, and build long-term protection for our relationship. Remember, pruning allows for more fruitfulness and the ability to carry a heavier load.

God also wanted to deal with our heart in our marriage, our thought life, and the vulnerability and honesty we really wanted and desired. He was putting on pressure and turning up the heat in the area of transparency in our marriage. If some find themselves in serious trouble in their marriages, transparency is the answer.

THE THOUGHTS AND INTENTS OF THE HEART

We have a million different thoughts that pass through our minds each day. Some are good and some are not so good. A preacher once asked the audience if we would be okay if he put all of our thoughts of the day on a movie screen for anyone to see. Would you be okay with that? We are accustomed to keeping our thoughts to ourselves, and to reveal those thoughts would be an invasion of our privacy. After all, we only disclose those thoughts that cause us to be perceived in a good light; we present who we want to be.

God shows us in Second Corinthians 10:5 that we are to bring *"every thought into captivity to the obedience of Christ."* Our thought life is not supposed to run rampant but is meant to be kept in check—there may even come a time when we are to share some thoughts with our spouse. James Robinson, in his book *Living in Love,* suggests, "Whenever your thoughts or actions would grievously hurt your spouse, you should confess them and deal with them openly and honestly. If you think your actions are all that matters, think again. Jesus plainly tells us that our thoughts and intentions are equally important: *'Anyone who even looks at a woman with lust has already committed adultery with her in his heart'* (Matthew 5:28 NLT). You can commit serious sin without ever acting on your thoughts, because God is always looking at your heart, not just at your outward actions (see 1 Sam. 16:7)."[4]

THE NEED FOR TRANSPARENCY

As I stated earlier, Adam and Eve walked naked (open and transparent) with each other before sin had entered into the Garden.

They had openness in every way. As soon as they sinned, however, they covered themselves up with fig leaves. They put on a protective layer to cover their nakedness, and the total openness and transparency was instantly gone. They would conceal rather than share, they would cover instead of confess, and they would blame and justify instead of taking ownership and being repentant.

We believe that the main reason God wanted to have us walk this out personally was not only to share hidden secrets from the past, but also to protect our future marriage by living this out on a regular basis. If this is not a part of your marriage today, we believe any couple can recover and have some of what Adam and Eve lost before the fall. Walking transparent lives is not easy, but it is the best way to live.

Transparency in marriage reveals who you are to your spouse—it gives them the full picture. The biggest hurdle in transparency is showing them the real you and taking the risk in wondering if they will still accept you. You must be willing to share your inner thoughts, struggles, and weaknesses. It's too easy just to share the good stories or the struggles that do not affect your spouse; but as soon as you enter into sharing the hidden sins and secrets that may affect your spouse, that is when most people would run from truth rather than expose themselves. We would also add that you must be willing to share feelings and thoughts more than just facts.

Honesty and trust are foundational requirements to have a strong and lasting marriage. Without these, a marriage has broken walls that give room to the enemy. Hiddenness opens the door to the enemy and allows for living separate lives. This is the opposite of face to face. Any area that is closed to your spouse is dangerous and leaves you unprotected.

The enemy may even try to console you by telling you that if you keep the secret it would be better, sharing may hurt your spouse too much, or they may leave you due to the gravity of the betrayal. He may also whisper that you may lose the power that you once had, or lose the image that you presented. The risk is high and the investment is great. We won't tell you that this is easy; it may be the most difficult thing you will ever have to do or live out. There is great risk, but with great risk comes a greater return.

LEARNING FROM CRISIS

In 2009, we wanted to go to a marriage conference ourselves to strengthen our relationship, but instead of going to an event we decided to host one. So with a small staff and volunteers, we put up a website, invited some guest speakers and worship teams, and had a marriage conference. We had a great weekend, and we know a lot of marriages were strengthened and impacted through it. We were not prepared for what would come months afterward, however.

We kept the website up with all its info, which included an email address where people could email us about the event (even though the event was now months over). We received several emails from women who were in an adulterous affair with a close friend, and a couple of them were involved in an adulterous affair with their pastor. Their main question was when the appropriate time would be to share with their husbands about the affair.

We all know that these affairs didn't just happen overnight. There were steps taken, beginning in the eyes, heart, and thought life; then, when the opportunity was presented, they took it. The protection of the marriage covenant is hinged upon regular communication and openness—without it a marriage is uncovered and exposed.

TRUTH IS TRUST

The main issue in sharing who you are and the things that you have done and will do in the future is telling the truth—the full truth. One time we were counseling a lady who said that she and her husband don't lie, they just exaggerate. We had to work hard at not laughing at such a comment. Lying is not telling the truth completely; a half-truth is not the whole truth. Exaggerated truth, or extending the lines of the situation, is not the whole truth either.

The main reason for sharing half-truths is to cover who we really are. Even hiding feelings of the moment is to conceal who we are in those moments. The world of thoughts and feelings is so real that to reveal them would be to expose so much of who we are. We don't want our spouses to know what our true weaknesses are and what areas we are susceptible to. We conceal because we want to protect ourselves. Some tend to be vague and elusive when sharing the issue that has surfaced; they would rather not disclose how it truly happened, with all the emotions and thoughts that went alongside it. Some may even share the emotions but share them in such a way that they would be perceived differently.

In First Corinthians 2:11, Paul asks a question that should cement the need for clear and unhindered communication: "Who knows the thoughts of a man?" The answer is only "the man's spirit within him." Paul urges us that no one can know what is really going on unless we let our spouse in by sharing our inmost feelings and thoughts. God wants our spouse to have full access to the heart and thoughts. After all, this is the whole you and the full truth of what took place; sharing creates a safe place for protection, safety, and accountability. Will you allow yourself to cover or be revealed? Will you allow your spouse all the way in, especially into the hardest and most intimate areas? Will you refuse to communicate or will you open the door to your heart?

Barry and Lori Byrne, in their book *Love After Marriage*, conclude that:

> As a couple, if you respond to your spouse out of fear in an attempt to avoid disapproval, you will create an environment that stifles your ability to know and truly see each other. But when you risk being honest, despite potential conflict, you set the stage for a safe and enjoyable relationship. There can also be a temptation to avoid truth by editing inward thoughts and feelings so that you are perceived in a particular way.... We need to find a way to accurately and kindly represent our inner thoughts and feelings in all of life so that we will not be tempted to varnish the truth when it counts the most.[5]

SPEAKING TRUTH IN LOVE

One of the greatest keys to intimacy in marriage is sharing truths in love. Paul said, *"But, speaking the truth in love, may grow up in all things into Him who is the head—Christ"* (Eph. 4:15). Verbal communication is essential to knowing each other. Truth speaking is the best nurturer for growth and strength in marriage for the long term, which leads to Christlikeness.

In Gary Chapman's book, *Now You're Speaking My Language*, he states, "When divorced couples were asked, 'Why did your marriage fail?' 86 percent said, 'Deficient communication.' If that is true, then communication in marriage must be extremely important."[6]

There must be a commitment made to walk in a truthful and vulnerable way. There must be a resolve that we won't withhold anything from one another, including thoughts and emotions. This becomes disheartening to walk out if only one spouse commits, while the other is not engaged or only halfhearted in it. Some people share their feelings easier than others, and some want to define vulnerability differently. Some will only share if things are "pulled" out of them. The resolution of both spouses to walk face to face and to commit to take initiative on their own without any pushing or prying from the other spouse is critical. It is imperative that both lead in this and both are resolved to turn their hearts toward each other and walk in intimacy. God will breathe on your marriage the greatest power and grace if both are committed to going into the hidden places of your hearts.

RUNNING FORWARD

In a marriage, you will be a part of both repenting and the forgiving. So remember that how you treat the other is going to come full circle. When you walk in confession, change of direction is imperative. If a person only confesses but doesn't change, it can potentially create more pain and distrust. Confession is not the end but only the beginning. Looking forward is turning from the past and practically and diligently walking this out. It is not an overnight change, but a step-by-step change.

In moving forward, there are some things that you can do to start sharing who you really are, as well as learning about your spouse. Here are some ideas to help you go deeper in your marriage relationship:

1. Pray together regularly. This has been one of the greatest strengthening agents for us in our own

marriage. When God is invited in as a part of your life, He will do what you cannot.

2. Talk about what you are learning. This can bring enjoyment and learning from each other. I heard from a father years ago to pay attention to what really excites your children; therein you get to learn who they really are. This is also true of your spouse. Paying attention to what excites and saddens them reveals a lot.

3. Talk about your children, family, or special relationships you share. In the journey of life, you get to enjoy different seasons. Share them, talk about them, and celebrate them. This is one of the greatest pleasures of life.

4. Talk about the spiritual state of your home. Is it dull in the things of God or alive in the things of God? Is it lukewarm, cold, or hot? This will lead to a lot more discussion and hopefully action.

5. Heart connect regularly on both the good and bad. Keep this simple. This is more than just talking about regular business life, such as bills, schedules, and work. Learn about each other.

6. If you're going to share something that is more of a sensitive, tender issue, we encourage that you set the time apart so that if you have kids they are not involved, and enough time to discuss issues is allotted.

7. Share everything all at once, including emotions and thought processes. This is part of sharing the

complete truth and allowing them into the whole of you. Avoid generalities and pat answers. Go past the surface. Go deep into the heart.

8. When discussing sensitive issues and giving and receiving potential hurt and pain, please remember to walk in humility and honor, repent quickly, and forgive quicker. Everyone responds to hurt and offense differently.

Even with everything we have been through, by our submission to God and His grace we have come out victorious. And you can too! Now is the time to begin to put into practice these ideas we've given you—today is the most significant day you have before you. Embrace the process. You can have a thriving marriage, living in a face-to-face relationship.

Chapter 5

THE GLORY OF FATHERS

A son's first hero, a daughter's first love.
—Unknown

While driving back to Minneapolis from a funeral in Wisconsin in 2009, I (Antonio) had a sudden and sobering epiphany about the people in my car. I lost my breath and was overwhelmed with the awesome image I saw in my rearview mirror. I saw my children and wife sleeping while I drove. My eyes could hardly contain my gratitude toward God for allowing me to be a husband and father caring for my family.

God calls people to different tasks, but He has called me to be a father and a husband above all else. He gave me a beautiful wife and children, and He has allowed me to feel His heart and passion in being their protector, their provider, their guide, and so much more. I looked back in the rearview mirror that day overcome by the grace of God in that He has allowed me to feel what He feels toward my family. These are my children, the fruit of my marriage. They are looking to me as their father. I began to cry and pray. I also began to thank God for each of their personalities, while waves of memories flooded my thoughts and emotions.

Proverbs 17:6 says, *"The glory of children is their father."* An earthly father shares the same title as God the Father, which is a very glorious and sacred title. From this title and identity, we get to experience what God feels as a Father toward His children. This title and position has been undermined and undervalued, and it now holds very little weight compared to God's original desire expressed in the Garden. In this hour, what we need is a revolution of leaders—men who will lead their homes spiritually, physically, and emotionally. We desperately need fathers today!

FATHERLESS HOMES

Loving our wives and training our children in the ways of the Lord are paramount to the success of the church of tomorrow. This current generation is essentially fatherless. Let me share with you some statistics of our present-day, fatherless generation.

Cheryl Wetzstein, in an article written for the *Washington Times*, writes:

> Many children today are being raised without a mother and a father in a single-parent family unit and are primarily raised by their mothers. In the United States, approximately 27% of children (19.8 million) live with only one parent, in most instances their mother (23% live with their mother but not fathers). This includes 50% of black children, 26% of Hispanic children, 17% of non-Hispanic white children and 8% of Asian children. Ten percent of children living with two parents (5.3 million) live with a biological parent and a

stepparent. Most of these children (4.1 million) live with their mother and a stepfather.[1]

However, there is more than one way to be fatherless. These statistics don't share the disastrous effects of an *absentee father.* Millions of children live with an absentee father who is mentally, emotionally, and even physically disconnected from his family, even if he still lives in the home. Dr. Ken Canfield, in his book *The 7 Secrets of Effective Fathers*, says, "It's actually impossible for a father to be truly absent; part of him is always there. But in the fatherless home, he has given up his right to represent himself, and he often gets translated into a ghost, or a haunting spirit, or some would say a demon. No statistic can adequately measure the amount of pain caused by an absent father."[2] The person with the most authority in a family is the husband and father. When the man of the house is not present, his absence will still govern the family structure.

God never intended things to be this way. The evil one has assaulted the very basis of the foundation in marriage; he is an expert at causing fathers and children to turn away from one another. The bloodiest and most violent battlefields in history were not in Japan and in France during World War II—they are in our homes, our bedrooms, and our minds at work. We must commit to faithfulness in marriage and in our homes now more than ever before.

It saddens me to say that even if a Christian father raises a child, they are often not taught the ways of the Lord. Even though this may sound like a mass generalization, many fathers look at their children as being nothing more than photo ops rather than children whom he should nurture, train, discipline, equip, love, and release. Children are a reward from God, an inheritance that we get to partake of on this side of Heaven (see Ps. 127:3). We desperately need a turning of the home today.

It is my personal belief that the enemy works extra hard to remove the strength of boys before they even grow up. He hates the family and marriage and women, but predominantly he hates the power and masculinity of men. If satan can't kill unborn boys, he will destroy them by taking away their fathers. Because men usually follow the example of the father they have seen while growing up, the enemy works to create an *absentee* father rather than a loving, time-giving, providing father.

If this approach doesn't work, satan will try to tempt the father with lust—he then becomes so broken and burdened with guilt and problems that when he *can* marry, he is living with too much self-hatred to be an effective leader. I see this as the strategy and plan of the devil.

THE WAR ON MEN

The greatest need of the hour in which we live is to have men— real men. We have a dilemma right now: we have a culture where boys are living in men's bodies. Our culture is filled with men who act like boys. Men are not leaving their childish ways behind as they grow into adulthood; they are not leading, giving, and serving. Instead, they are taking, using, and abandoning. Not only that, but more and more women are enabling this in men. Mothers are enabling their boys to stay boys, even when they are 25 years old and their wives don't know what to do with them, because they think this is normal. This epidemic is definitely not normal! We need a biblical understanding of manhood that challenges the status quo.

A major reason for this dilemma of men acting like boys is that society has been trying to make men into girls. The feminist movement has been trying to raise up women to become men and men to become women. There have been countless articles, books, and interviews on this subject that have had catastrophic effects. Looking back at it now, we can see that what the radical feminists tried to do in many ways was successful. The feminist movement is undergirded with vengeful hate. There is a strong, underlying hatred of men who operate in a position of leadership, provision, and responsibility, which comes from a hate rooted in a deep, specific source—somehow there was hurt initiated by a particular man, such as a father, a husband, a boyfriend, a boss, or a teacher. This hatred is amplified in sex, in childrearing, and in the workplace.

A feminist would get angry toward the biblical principles that God has given to both man and woman—He appointed man to lead, govern, and protect, while giving women the awesome responsibility to help lead, support, and nurture. Feminists have warped and twisted what God created as good and made it out instead to be wrong and discriminatory. While it may be true that men, as human beings, have abused their God-given authority, we don't throw out what God has created as the structure for safety and strength and try to flip it upside down while demonizing the gender itself. This is exactly what feminism has done; it has col-lapsed the God-given strength of the family.

One of the early feminists was Gloria Steinem, founder of the National Organization for Women and editor of *Ms.* magazine. Here is a sample of her perspective on childrearing:

> We've had a lot of people in this country who have had the courage to raise their daughters more like their sons, which is great because it means they're more equal.... But there are fewer people who have had the

courage to raise their sons more like their daughters. And that's what needs to be done.[3]

One of the major goals of feminism is to make men and women equal in every way. It began with the notion that women should have the same authority and responsibility as a man. Feminists were sick of men's entitlement and women's submission. Their fear was that women would somehow be less human if they chose to stay at home with their children instead of pursuing a career. Somehow, to their way of thinking, being out of the home was a way of achieving equal status with men. They began to desire the same jobs, salary, and education that men had. Not only that, when women became educated, they didn't want to serve men in lower-level jobs, such as secretarial work; they wanted the higher profile, upper-management positions at the top of the working world. We look around us today and see that the feminist ideals have translated into reality.

Hanna Rosin, another feminist liberal, shares some current facts on the workplace. In 2010, Rosin headlined the first TED women's conference, held in Washington, D.C. She said, "We are going through an unprecedented moment, where the power dynamics of men and women are shifting very rapidly...for every two men that get a college degree, three women will do the same. Women for the first time this year became the majority of the American workforce...over 50% of managers are women...in this global economy, women are more successful than men. These economic changes are rapidly affecting our culture. What our romantic comedies look like, and our new set of superheroes... wives begin to take over as top family earners."[4]

At the heart of this is the feminist desire to absolutely eliminate any differences between a man and a woman, a boy or a girl. They even addressed the "problem" of "sexism" in children's toys. Germaine Greer, a dominant voice in the feminist upheaval, said, "So where does the difference (between the sexes) come from? If it's all bred into us by people like toy makers, who steer boys toward these trucks, girls to the dolls, and by the teachers, parents, employers—all the wicked influencers of a sexist society—then maybe this is a social problem that needs to be fixed."[5] Consequently, toy stores were pressured through various avenues, including the media, court cases, and psychiatrists, to "fix" the "sexist" problem. Many toy stores "implemented a 'gender neutral' approach to marketing as demanded by feminists."[6]

The natural inclinations of a boy wanting to play with toy cars and girls with dolls and play houses were under attack. Why was natural biological preference such an issue? The feminists wanted to create feminine boys and masculine girls—they wanted girls to finally *be in charge.*

Even though retailers went back to organizing separate toy sections for boys and girls, the ideas that were initiated in the 60s and 70s have affected our culture forever. In our culture today there is a sweeping and aggressive attack on gender roles, creating the idea that parents can select the gender of their child. James Dobson writes, "There is a new source of confusion emanating from the powerful gay and lesbian agenda. Its propagandists are teaching a revolutionary view of sexuality called 'gender feminism,' which insists that sex assignment is irrelevant. Genetics can be simply overridden. What matters is the 'gender' selected for us by parents when we are babies, or the sex role we choose for ourselves later in life."[7]

All-gender bathrooms on school campuses and public buildings are being legislated all across the United States. In 2013, Michael Nutter, the mayor of Philadelphia, signed a piece of legislation requiring that all bathrooms be gender-neutral in city-owned buildings.[8]

All of this has caused so much confusion in our culture today. Men and women's roles have been reversed from God's original structure. God has made men to take on a specific role, and He has created women to be unique and to function in a different role. This beautiful difference is foundational to marriage, so that when a man and a woman marry, they complement each other. What we don't want is to lose what God has given to us in creating *both* male and female, *both* boys and girls. Let's examine how God has made men to function as a source of strength.

MASCULINITY RESTORED

I have a son named Elijah. He is all boy. In fact, he is one of the most driven boys I have ever seen, even though all four of my sons are instinctively risk takers, inherently protective, excessively competitive, and willing to fight for a worthy cause.

While we were on a family trip, we stopped at a hotel that had a pool with a water slide, so all the kids went swimming. Elijah, who couldn't swim at the time, didn't want to be left out just because he was only five years old. He wanted to go down the slide like his older brothers, but the lifeguard on duty said he couldn't unless he could swim the entire width of the pool. Unbeknownst to us, he thought about it for a second and determined it was worth the risk. He jumped into the pool. He swam from side to side, the entire width of the pool. He came out and looked at the lifeguard, who gave Elijah a thumbs up. He was then able to go down the water slide by himself.

It's not uncommon in our family to have a race while we eat dinner or to run to the car to beat the person standing next to us. Every one of my children ran after balls since they were little and still love to play nonstop with them. After watching a fighting movie, they love to imitate the fighting moves. And they especially love superhero movies. My oldest son, Michael, from the time he was one until he was six, would take off his clothes to his underwear, ask me or his mom to tie a cape around his neck, and grab a sword. For the next hour he became a fighting superhero.

Here are some ways that boys, youth, and men instinctively have a desire to love, protect, provide, and give. These are examples from my own life. No one told me to do these things—I just inherently did them.

Conquest of my bride-to-be: When I was just 15 years old, during halftime at a basketball game, I stood up on a chair and said to the basketball players and attendees that I wanted to sing a song to my girl. I nervously sang a love song to Christelle, "Right Here Waiting" by Richard Marx. This was a risk for me, but I wanted to show off to Christelle in saying that I would do anything to romance her.

Protector of my bride: During our honeymoon, when I was only 19 years old, Christelle and I were walking on the street in the Cayman Islands. I heard some guys whistling at my new bride, making all sorts of crude comments to her. Without any hesitation, while holding Christelle's hand, I walked up to the four guys and said, "Who said that to my girl?" The three other guys fearfully pointed to the guy who said it. I looked at him with fiery eyes and an angry face, "If you don't say sorry to my girl, I will beat you to shreds!"

The guy who insulted and whistled at her immediately apologized, "Ah...ah...ah...I'm sorry." Although today I may take a different approach, considering how foolish my actions were at the time, I just wanted to show my new bride that I was going to protect her. I really was willing to risk my life for her.

The heart of a provider: After being married for a few weeks, Christelle and I moved into a fully furnished rental home. We didn't need to buy anything; in fact, we couldn't use any of our wedding gifts. Then, after six months, we found a duplex close to work and the university that I attended. We were so excited, but we didn't have any furniture to move with us. We window-shopped for a couple of weeks and knew what we wanted and needed to fill our new place, but we didn't have the money to do so. I saved as much money as I could and decided to surprise Christelle with a new kitchen table that we could eat from. I still remember that table today—it had white tile with wood edging, and it extended on both sides to seat up to six people. After work one Friday, I bought it and carried it into our new place. I was so excited to provide this for my wife. I could hardly carry it in. It took all of my strength and the vision of her excitement to carry it in. Then I brought her home later that day and showed it to her. She loved it! That day I felt what it was to provide for my wife and future family.

These are images and pictures of a man. Men are innately designed by our Creator God to lead a family, to risk our own safety for our family's protection, and to provide for those we love, all the while undergirded by the desire to serve our wives and family. John Piper and Wayne Grudem write in *Recovering Biblical Manhood and Womanhood*, "At the heart of mature masculinity is a sense of benevolent responsibility to lead, provide for and protect women in ways appropriate to a man's differing relationships."[9] A man may not feel a sense of responsibility; he may not know he's supposed to lead, provide, and protect. This is a good sign that he is immature in his masculinity and needs to be trained.

Wayne Grudem says some strong and clear statements that I fully agree with:

> Mature masculinity expresses itself not in the demand to be served, but in the strength to serve and to sacrifice for the good of woman. Jesus said, "Let the greatest among you become as the youngest and the leader as one who serves" (see Luke 22:26). Leadership is not a demanding demeanor. It is moving forward to a goal. If the goal is holiness and Heaven, the leading will have the holy aroma of Heaven about it—the demeanor of Christ. Thus after saying that "the husband is the head of the wife as Christ is the head of the church," Paul said, "Husbands, love your wives as Christ loved the church and gave himself up for her, that he might sanctify her" (see Ephesians 5:23,25-26). Jesus led his bride to holiness and Heaven on the Calvary road. He looked weak, but he was infinitely strong in saying NO to the way of the world. So it will be again and again for mature men as they take up the responsibility to lead.[10]

Men are not born leaders; they are trained to become leaders. Men don't fall into knowing how to lead by happenstance; they have to be taught by example and then be given the opportunity. Men have two main objectives that characterize them in leadership. Our aim is to be men like Jesus who are strong and aggressive in our effort to create a place of safety for women and children in a world where they struggle to find it. We are to be gentle and kind with our wives and children, loving our wives through the sacrificial love of a life laid down, like Jesus did for His bride. We are to be gentle leaders for our kids, letting them know they are gifts from God who we love and value greatly.

Jesus is our great example on how to be men and how to lead our wives. To be tough and tender is to be like Jesus as He is described in the book of Revelation: both as a Lion and as a Lamb (see Rev. 5:5-6). Commenting on these verses, John Piper writes, "A lion is admirable for its ferocious strength and imperial appearance. A lamb is admirable for its meekness and servant-like provision of wool for our clothing. But even more admirable is a lion-like lamb and a lamb-like lion."[11]

This is where we are right now. Men are to leave childish ways behind and lead, serve, and provide, giving of themselves for someone else. We must leave a lasting legacy for the next generation. We are meant to conquer battles and provide for our families. We are to love and cherish our wives and serve them with everything within us. Boys are meant to follow men and be trained by men. We are in grave need of this because so much is hinged on the role of men to lead, provide, and serve like Jesus.

I started from the basic masculinity crisis and established the foundation of being a man first, so that we may understand what it is to be a good father. As Jesus is our example to be a man, God the Father is the greatest example of how to be a father. Scripture reveals to us the heart of the Father, not formulas that explain what He does. God wants to show us His heart, His emotions, and His affections so that we may understand why He acts the way He does, more than just know about what He does.

There is no one more distinct on this earth than a father; just the very sound of one of my children yelling "Dad" is one of the most precious things in my life. From the time I set my eyes on the heartbeat of my first baby at the doctor's office, I had an amazing inner knowledge and experience of being a father. There is nothing else like it in this world. If you are a father, Ken Canfield writes, "You have been uniquely placed in the role of father of your children. Your wife may mother them, their teachers may mentor them, their coaches may train them, the government may foster them, but good fathering is needed in its own right."[12]

Identity Established from Their Fathers

Founder. Source. Chief. Leader. This is what the word *father* means. When one speaks of the father of a nation, or of a movement, or of a company, they are speaking of the one who helped bring it into being.[13] Our heavenly Father is the source from which all other things come into existence. Both statistically and scripturally, children learn who they are from their fathers—the father establishes the child's identity. Not only that, but blessings and curses come on us directly from our fathers (see Josh. 24:15). God created fatherhood with an eternal purpose—to reveal and represent Himself.

When a child looks at his earthly father, he should be able to see qualities of God the Father, which include:

- A loving provider

- A strong protector

- A truthful leader

- A respectable authority

- An intimate friend

Seeing these qualities in fathers affects how a child thinks about Father God. How we live as fathers will directly affect how a child's identity will be established and how they will view God the Father. For the rest of the chapter, I want to highlight some values that God wants men to follow in leading. I don't believe formulas or steps will work, even though we can learn from them. I believe God shows us His heart and His values and gives us a command to follow Him.

THE CORE OF THE ISSUE: VALUES OF FATHERS

Like spokes in a wheel, at the very heart of a family is the father. Men are always leading, but the question is, where are you leading? Where are you going? For where you go, the home goes too. Everything revolves around the father. We can learn a lot from surveying the Old Testament Scriptures on how the eastern cultures viewed the father.

Israelite families traced their official descent through the line of their father, and he was in charge of the household. Furthermore, when women married, they became a part of their husband's household. The term *patriarchy* has long defined the Israelite family structure. However, because *patriarchy* means "rule of the father," feminism has given it a negative connotation and even discredited it. The term *patricentrism*, which means "centered around the father," may better define the Israelite family. But this is not to say that the husband was to be a dictator; in fact, while Scripture refers to the father as the ruler of his household, it rarely focuses on the father's power. Within a healthy household, the father and husband was the one to inspire trust and security of his family.[14]

So much is centered on the need and integrity of the father today. Not only do boys become men by imitating their fathers, but daughters also need strong father figures in their lives so that they become healthy young women. Dr. Meg Meeker, from her book *Strong Fathers, Strong Daughters*, writes about the way girls are made:

> I have watched daughters talk to fathers. When you come into the room, they change. Everything about them changes: their eyes, their mouths, their gestures, their body language. Daughters are never lukewarm in the presence of their fathers. They might take their mothers for granted, but not you. They light up—or they cry. They watch you intensely. They hang on your words. They hope for your attention, and they wait for it in frustration—or in despair. They need a gesture of approval, a nod of encouragement, or even simple eye contact to let them know you care and are willing to help. When she's in your company, your daughter tries harder to excel. When you teach her, she learns more rapidly. When you guide her, she gains confidence. If you fully understood just how profoundly you can influence your daughter's life, you would be terrified, overwhelmed, or both. Boyfriends, brothers, even husbands can't shape her character the way you do. You will influence her entire life because she gives you an authority she gives no other man.[15]

LOVE GOD

Loving God is paramount for everything to flow from. In fact, it takes God to love God. We often think that loving God comes naturally, but really loving God is the result of knowing how He is moved by us, how He feels about us, and how He is passionate about us. Understanding God's deep emotion toward us causes our hearts to abound in love right back to Him. When asked what the greatest commandment was, Jesus responded:

> *"You shall love the Lord your God with all your heart, with all your soul, and with all your mind." This is the first and great commandment. And the second is like it: "You shall love your neighbor as yourself"* (Matthew 22:37-39).

Many men do not pursue a relationship with God simply because it is work (physical and spiritual labor), it requires intimacy with God and your wife, and it requires humility. Many men deal with shame, which is really an issue of unworthiness and feeling unqualified. These are all lies from the enemy that can and must be overturned. Every child is looking for a father, protector, and supporter. Even in weakness, there is no father like you—no one who is more anointed to lead your family, your Garden of Eden, than you.

Today, God is calling men into intimacy with Himself above all. We are not to hide behind our wives; we are to pursue a life with God that will overflow into having loving leadership in our homes. This is the greatest privilege we can have as men, for there is no greater honor than to tenderly guide, protect, and lead our families. Loving God is the basis and the foundation from which everything else will flow. We must pursue love above all!

LOVE YOUR WIFE (THE MOTHER OF YOUR CHILDREN)

The second most important thing to do to be a successful father is to love your wife. It is the greatest gift a child can receive—knowing his father loves his mother. Paul again admonishes us as men:

> *Husbands, love your wives, just as Christ also loved the church and gave Himself for her.... So husbands*

ought to love their own wives as their own bodies; he who loves his wife loves himself. For no one ever hated his own flesh, but nourishes and cherishes it, just as the Lord does the church (Ephesians 5:25,28-29).

God is calling husbands to love the women we married in a self-sacrificial way! We are to love our wives as Christ loved the church, which was without limits. He chose to lay down His life for her. This means we are to sacrifice every day for our wives.

As husbands, we are called to put to death our own selfish desires to meet our wife's deepest needs. Christ's love for the church is based upon His choice, commitment, and unchanging character, not on us. God loves us not because we are lovable, but because He is so loving. There is nothing that we can do to generate more love from Him or to take His love away from us, because it was never based upon us to begin with. So maintain an unwavering commitment to your wife; love and cherish her in secret and in public. It is not good enough to create some sort of public façade for others to see when it is not what you live out in the home.

The responsibility for building a family in the ways of the Lord begins with the husband's treatment of his wife. Everything hinges upon this. If the husband does not serve and cherish his wife, he will not have a spirit of prayer upon his life. This is why prayer rooms of the earth are predominantly made up of women. Without a spirit of prayer upon a man, the effectiveness of the family will be greatly reduced. Peter writes:

Husbands, likewise, dwell with them with understanding, giving honor to the wife, as to the weaker vessel, and as being heirs together of the grace of life, that your prayers may not be hindered (1 Peter 3:7).

Scripture calls us to understand and honor our wives as equal partners or heirs in the Kingdom of God. Any man who fails to do this will be hindered in his prayer life. We must give her equal respect in the Kingdom as co-heirs in the grace of God. Growing in prayer is linked to honoring and understanding women. The prayer movement is a movement to honor marriage. Husbands are to commit to understanding and honoring their wives, regardless of how they feel about them romantically.

TURNING OF THE HEART

Behold, I will send you Elijah the prophet before the coming of the great and dreadful day of the Lord. And he will turn the hearts of the fathers to the children, and the hearts of the children to their fathers, lest I come and strike the earth with a curse (Malachi 4:5-6).

The Lord is restoring fatherhood as the foundation of maturity. Malachi defines God's promised restoration specifically as restoring fathers to children and children to their fathers. At the heart of the Gospel is a heavenly Father who wants a family, and a heavenly Bridegroom who wants a bride. Restored families are a key strategy in God's restoration of people, the church, and society.

TRAINING OUR CHILDREN

In every generation, the fathers' ability to train their children determines the success or failure of the church, and the condition of the church determines the success or failure of society. The Lord wants to turn our hearts toward Him. Moses reminded the Israelites:

And these words which I command you today shall be in your heart. You shall teach them diligently to your children, and shall talk of them when you sit in your house, when you walk by the way, when you lie down, and when you rise up (Deuteronomy 6:6-7).

As fathers we must ask the Lord to turn our hearts toward our children. The Lord is inviting us into a season of prayer, reflection, repentance, and acts of love. We must ask the Lord to give us His heart for our children. There is a required turning. Most generations are willing to sell out their children's legacy for their short-term gratification (see 2 Kings 20; Isa. 39:6-8).

We must turn our hearts toward our children by understanding the importance of building a family altar. Abraham walked the land and built altars of worship that attracted the presence of God to the land. In fact, throughout Genesis, the children of Israel encountered God in the very locations where Abraham had built altars unto the Lord.

We want to build altars of worship in our homes that attract the presence of God and lead our children into encounters with God. Isaac, Jacob, and Joseph had encounters and dreams in places where Abraham had previously worshiped. This should give us a vision for how significant our leadership is within the home. As a father goes, so goes the generation. Let's ask God for the kind of vision that will impact our entire lineage.

TEACHING YOUR CHILDREN

The grand design instituted by God is for the father to teach and lead his family and his grandchildren into God's ways. The children's character should be distinguished by the fear of the Lord. Again, Moses said:

And these words which I command you today shall be in your heart. You shall teach them diligently to your children, and shall talk of them when you sit in your house, when you walk by the way, when you lie down, and when you rise up. You shall bind them as a sign on your hand, and they shall be as frontlets between your eyes. You shall write them on the doorposts of your house and on your gates (Deuteronomy 6:6-9).

God begins by instructing the father first: He commands the father to *"love the Lord your God with all your heart, with all your soul, and with all your strength"* (Deut. 6:5). This protects the father's heart as he puts God first in his life. It's like the training we get for emergency procedures as we take off in a commercial plane. If the plane is having problems, a mask will deploy and we are urged to place the mask on ourselves first and then help those around us. Loving God first and keeping His commands will stop a father from telling the kids one thing and then doing something else. Hypocrisy will only lead the children into confusion and into paths that take them away from God. We can't live by the old saying, "Do as I say, not as I do."

The second command that God gives to fathers regarding their children is to "teach them diligently." Diligence is characterized by being consistent, earnest, and steady. The Word of God should be reiterated and repeated constantly within our homes. Fathers are to rehearse God's ways to their children. This command presumes that teachers know their content, which in turn presumes concentrated effort and study. This is especially important for the father because it's so easy for him to want to disconnect from the family. One of the weaknesses of man is to become lazy. But God commands fathers to lead their children in the ways of God diligently.

Next, Scripture exhorts fathers to *"talk of them when you sit in your house, when you walk by the way, when you lie down, and when you rise up."* Teaching God's ways should be a regular part of a family's daily life and activities. Moses uses sitting and walking, lying down and rising up to suggest that any time is appropriate for instruction in the ways of the Lord. God's words are the touchstone in which to guide our children's lives, and we are to speak of God's ways all day long.

God ends by saying you are to *"bind them as a sign on your hand, and they shall be as frontlets between your eyes. You shall write them on the doorposts of your house and on your gates."* This Scripture refers to speaking, looking for, and seeing images of God's ways throughout our daily lives. These words are figurative, or course, and denote an undeviating observance of God's ways and commands. Every aspect of your home should show reverence for God's righteous ways, His glory, and His majesty.

The Word of God should be reflected in our homes. When our family comes into our home, when they watch TV, when they go to their bedrooms, when they enter the kitchen, and when they work or play on the computer—the Word of God should be evident. Our family should see the Word of God ever before them. Our homes should be a place where they learn God's ways, all day long and in every room.

PROPHETIC HISTORY

As a father, do you have a prophetic history and are you forming a prophetic history with your family? Is your family tracing the beautiful line of God's redemptive hand? Are you building altars of worship where your children and grandchildren can encounter God? We are to foster a heart attitude that cultivates a prophetic, watchful spirit. Fathers are to hear what the Spirit is saying to their families. I've seen many homes where the wife is prophetically sharp but the husband has a dull, lethargic spirit. This has to change. We have no idea of the power of a father with a watchful spirit.

Fathers must accept the primary responsibility of training and equipping our children in the ways of the Lord. We are not to wait for a church program to reform our wayward children. Gone are the days where this will even have any significant impact. The world is discipling our children—schools have our children 40 hours a week. On average, children are watching 44.5 hours of various screens, including television, movies, and the Internet.[16] How can we expect one hour of Sunday school to have a significant impact in their lives? God never intended this to be the model for our homes.

Leading your home is like leading a government. Jonathan Edwards said, "Every Christian family ought to be as it were a little church, consecrated to Christ, and wholly influenced and governed by his rules. And family education and order are some of the chief of the means of grace."[17] Edwards would regularly lead his family in prayer and reading of the Word, where "a chapter in the Bible was read, commonly by candle light in the winter; upon which he asked his children questions according to their age and capacity; and took occasion to explain some passages, or enforce any dully recommended."[18]

THE ADMONITION OF THE LORD

Paul only gives two admonitions to fathers in the New Testament. He repeats the first one twice, exhorting fathers not to provoke their children to wrath (see Eph. 6:4; Col. 3:21). Fathers are tempted to enforce obedience through severity and a display of anger (which is really intimidation or a spirit of rebellion). The second reference is to "bring up your children in the training and admonition of the Lord."

We must teach our children how to pray and worship through relationship, which is something shown more than told. It's critical to continually look for ways to encourage your children to live out their Christian walk as a normal part of life. This lifestyle means more than just attending regularly scheduled religious events. One of the most effective ways I have found to invite my kids into learning to walk out their faith is to give them faith heroes to look up to. Sharing testimonies of how God moved in my life and inviting my kids to pray with the family about everyday things has been a powerful way to develop our family relationships and our relationship with God.

LEADING THROUGH OUR OWN WEAKNESS

During the Christmas season, our family enjoys relaxing, playing games, watching movies, and eating—lots and lots of eating! One particular Christmas we watched a lot of Christmas movies that were good, clean family entertainment. Then we began adding episodes of *Little House on the Prairie* and *Leave It to Beaver*. We had made it a priority to watch movies that upheld good values, even if the culture around us may have thought that they were "old school." Our family really enjoyed it! But what happened as a result of that time was that we became dull and disconnected from the life of God. We weren't watching anything wrong or bad. That was not the point. We had prayed less and less and read the Bible less and less. Our family time with God had become less of a priority.

When we went back to the flow of ministry, Christelle and I felt the lack in our sensitivity to the Holy Spirit. We weren't as vibrant as we felt we should be. We discussed this and made a decision to speak to our children and make some changes. We felt we needed to change our focus on entertainment; even if it wasn't wrong, it did take away from the vibrant spirit and sensitivity to God that we wanted for our whole family.

As a father, I brought our family together and shared with them the new direction we were going to go. I apologized for allowing the amount (quantity) of entertainment played in our home and the lack of our time with God. I also began to share with them about the lives of Charles Finney, John G. Lake, and Evan Roberts. I highlighted Evan Roberts, who was only 26 years old when revival broke out, and who had several encounters with God while he was younger. I also shared with them that the disciples Jesus walked with were young men and not old as many suppose. More than likely, they were only about 17–24 years old. I told them that they can encounter God, even at their young age, and that they can do great exploits, just as those other young men did. God is the same yesterday, today, and tomorrow. What God invites us into is faith and a desperate desire for His presence.

What transpired within our family was truly awesome. After we discussed these things together, the kids went to bed. Two of our older boys began to get a vision for revival and a hunger for prayer and encountering God. So they got out of bed and began praying, being touched by the Holy Spirit and crying out for God's presence. They were up for three hours in prayer, reading, and spending time with God. I could barely get out of them the next day the experience they had.

MISSIONARY LIFE

Missionary families do everything together. What I mean by that is that you take your kids with you wherever you go, not as a cute thing, but as an integral part of doing the Lord's will together as a family. This is part of teaching and training. My wife and I took our family around the world as missionaries for over ten years. I want to encourage you to embrace a missionary life as well.

Years ago I knew that I wanted my children to know not only what I did publicly, but how I did it. I remember when I first got into ministry that I desperately wanted to be trained. I learn best when I am watching someone else, instead of when someone is just telling me what to do. So I began to imitate those I respected. I watched how they said things and learned why they did certain things. I copied what I saw, so I knew that my kids could learn by watching and ministering with me.

Another part to embracing a missionary life is to have your kids pray over you, study the Word, and teach you about subjects. We have to provoke them into the things of God, not just assume that they will get it. I not only want to teach them principles of the Word of God, but I want them to know how to teach the Word of God to others and their own families one day.

During these leadership-training times, they are going to teach our family the Bible. We exhort them that they must learn to research, study, and dig for themselves. We have periodically done exercises where we invite the kids to grab a theme and stand up and teach the Word of God to us, with practical applications that show how that truth is personal to them. Then they pray over us, imparting that truth to us. This has been a fun yet learning time of finding out how much our kids know about the Word. We give them feedback, encouraging them and watching them grow into men and women of God in the safest place we can have—our home.

SUMMARY

In closing, there are many things to be said of the glory of being a father who represents the greatest father—God. We can learn a lot from what He feels, what He does, and what He inspires us to be like. The father's role is very significant for the health of the family and for the good of society. The father is designed by God to fulfill two things:

1. Confirm gender identity: God chose at conception from the seed of the father to determine the gender of a child.

2. Release into identity: fathers tend to focus on release.

I started this chapter by sharing the crisis that we are in, where men are degraded and emasculated to the point where they are shamed and cannot be the good fathers they were created to be. I urge you to look at any areas in your life where you may have suffered the effects of this crisis.

I like to look at my family as a submarine already in the water, in the midst of a great battle. Some days are peaceful and others are a full attack from the enemy. I recognize and see the "holes" in my submarine, holes where I need God's grace and strength to lead my family. Like many men, I can see these holes that are letting in water.

The question for you is, *Where are the holes in your home? Do you want to stop sinking, or will you continue to be distracted and let the enemy take and divide your family?* Some of you reading this may be new fathers who want to be proactive in not allowing any holes to form, while others reading these words are already sinking. Your heart is already saying, "God, help me!" If that's you, whatever season or circumstance you find yourself in, God's grace is sufficient. If you're married, God gave you your great helper, your wife. She will help you and is perfectly compatible with strengths where you are lacking. Together, you're a force to be reckoned with. Rely on God to help you close and seal up those holes. Let Him help you aim your offensive torpedoes at your enemy.

In conclusion, I urge you to make a vow and a recommitment to lead your wife and family in God's ways. Here are some suggestions:

- As a husband and father, I vow to have regular times of prayer and reading of the Word with my family.

- As a husband and father, I commit to following God's ways. I choose to close doors and windows that have allowed the enemy to have a foothold in my home.

- As a husband and father, I commit to walking humbly, serving, and caring for my wife and children. I will protect, provide, and give of my life to build a legacy that will be fruitful and full of life for generations after me.

God has anointed you to lead your family. Now it's time to lead and teach the next generation of God's goodness.

Chapter 6

EMBRACING MOTHERHOOD

My deepest sense of "fulfillment," my highest human joys, have been found in being a wife and a mother.
—ELISABETH ELLIOT*

What it means to embrace motherhood has been something that I (Christelle) have been pondering in my heart for many years. I do not want to call it just "motherhood," because a woman can be a mother, and even a good one at that, without really embracing it.

The moment I gave birth to our first beautiful son, I hoped that somehow I could change the world by investing in this little life one moment at a time—but could I really? As the realities of how much work and time it took to raise a child set in, my dreams of raising kids who changed the world dwindled to hoping I could get enough free time to take a shower. My new-mom excitement slowly evolved into fighting to keep my attitudes in check as I walked around on little sleep, wondering why my husband didn't seem to get it. I worked through many feelings and emotions, trying to use the Word of God as my guide. I kept reminding myself that I must do this as "unto the Lord," and I desperately tried to keep my heart free of a "complaining spirit," with some success.

By the time we had our third son, I was getting used to constant nursing, sleepless nights, and a messy house, but was I "embracing motherhood" or just getting through it? I knew children were a blessing, but did I really believe that? How would I raise kids to be equipped to live a life of radical obedience to the Lord in a culture that pursues mostly personal gain instead of sacrifice? If being a mother was so valuable, then why did society treat it as a downgrade for women? Why do cultural norms, even in Christian circles, seem to be so very different from Scripture? Can being a mom really affect the Kingdom more than pursuing my own interests, even if they are godly ones? Do I have what it takes to raise kids as ammunition against the enemy, as Psalm 127:4 says?

As our family continued to grow, I began to ask God to reveal the answers to these questions. God has since allowed me a glimpse of what I get to take part in by being a mother. I am not only getting to raise five children who pursue God and take hold of what He has for them, but I am building a legacy that will echo throughout all eternity.

A woman is the only one who has the awesome privilege of holding within her a miraculous life that is an eternal being created in God's image. She was chosen by God to bring forth a soul into the world through her own flesh, which is both flesh and eternal. This astounding fact alone establishes the incredible glory that motherhood is.

We all have a deep desire within us to live a life that lasts for eternity. We want our life to make a difference in the life of others.

Motherhood is the most practical arena in which we can do this, yet it is so often overlooked and undervalued.

We run a discipleship training school called the Pursuit Internship. This internship was birthed out of our passion and obedience to disciple all nations, as Jesus commanded (see Matt. 25). We work hard to see that our students get the training, speaking, and the mentoring they need to truly know Christ for themselves and make Him known in the earth. We give our time, energy, and passion to provide an atmosphere where godly character can develop and where they can effectively go forth into the earth on their own, making disciples themselves. The opportunity to train these students in our ministry internship is both wonderful and powerful, but it is nothing compared to the opportunity we have as parents with our kids, and more specifically the one we have as mothers. Our kids have an "internship" with us in our home. They learn what they will use for the rest of their lives from us.

I remember one day sitting with my kids building Legos on the floor when I looked at them and saw within them the budding virtue and the opportunity I had to shape their little minds and lives for Jesus. I have five kids to whom I have unlimited access, to instill whatever I want. This incredible responsibility also carries with it an immense amount of opportunity and excitement. When we begin to get a vision for how to disciple our children, it fills the daily processes of life with purpose.

WOMEN ARE NURTURERS

Women are nurturers by God-given design, whether or not we have one child through our physical bodies. Elisabeth Elliot, in her book *Let Me Be a Woman*, writes:

The body of every normal woman prepares itself repeatedly to receive and to bear. Motherhood requires self-giving, sacrifice, suffering. It is going down into death in order to give life, a great human analogy of a great spiritual principle. Womanhood is a call. It is a vocation to which we respond under God, glad if it means the literal bearing of children, thankful as well for what it means in a much wider sense, that in which every woman, married or single, fruitful or barren, may participate—the unconditional response exemplified for all time in Mary the virgin, and the willingness to enter into suffering, to receive, to carry, to give life, to nurture and to care for others.[1]

One day when our daughter Isabella was about four years old, I was cleaning the house when I distinctly noticed something unusual—*silence*. As silence is something that is rare in our bustling house of seven, I proceeded to find out what our kids were doing and where exactly they were. I was yelling her name when she quickly came out of her room and said, "Shhhh. Mommy, the babies are going to sleep." I opened the door to find the light off, blinds shut, nightlight on, and a row of dolls and stuffed animals covered with blankets. Even her brother Justice, who was a baby at the time, was on the floor covered with a blanket as he looked up at me and grinned, enjoying the *mothering* he was receiving from his big sister. I think many of us have stories similar to this one.

In fact, the times I have witnessed a scene like this one either from me doing it as a little girl, or the times I babysat or saw my younger sisters do this, are numerous and probably couldn't be counted, even if I tried. Even with the varying ethnicities and personalities the women over the globe exemplify, the fact is that we as woman are nurturers from birth. No matter what we do, we *mother* and it is our function, our greatest strength, and a powerful gift given to us by God. We are anointed to mother.

The word *mother* means to give birth to, to create and produce; to watch over, nourish, and protect maternally.[2] The meaning of the word *mother* is full of richness and depth, and it gives us a key to our purpose and calling in life. It distinguishes our giftings from the giftings of men and reveals part of the reason we feel and express ourselves so differently than men do. The innate desires within us that this mothering instinct produces are timeless and are the ways we express ourselves in life.

SUSANNA WESLEY

Remember your leaders, who spoke the word of God to you. Consider the outcome of their way of life and imitate their faith (Hebrews 13:7 NIV).

Some years ago as Antonio and I began to read and study the history of the great awakenings and revivals, a few thoughts came to me. Who were the mothers of the many great men and women who changed history for Jesus? What kinds of families did these men and women come from? What were the key factors for those who brought revival and awakening to many nations across the earth? These and many questions like them arose as we were reading and studying the revivals of the history of the church. If these key figures were used so mightily, what in their life was key to their passion and resolve?

There are many answers and conclusions we came to, but one woman stood out to me in my quest for answers—Susanna Wesley. Susanna, born in 1669, was the wife of Samuel Wesley and a mother of 19 children (10 of whom died). She is perhaps best known for being the mother of John and Charles Wesley. To these two sons we can attribute the birth of the great Methodist revival, which not only affected England but also the Great Awakenings in America. Their stance for truth in the face of persecution does not even begin to give us an understanding of the ripple effect just these two men's lives had on the world. Their lives were abandoned for Christ and changed the face of Christianity. They remain today examples for us to follow, and we may never know until eternity the contributions these two men brought to Christianity and to history.

Susanna was a devout Christian and made it her aim to see that her children were trained up in Scripture and the ways of the Lord. She was diligent, hardworking, and resourceful. She lived her life with deep conviction, and it was evident she lived before the eyes of God. Susanna was a woman of high education, which was rare in her time, and she used her education to see that her children were raised to be followers of Christ. A simple study reveals her passion and priority to her children's spiritual condition. She was a woman who saw more than just her own life or even her children's lives; she saw into the future, and she had vision. One quote from John Wesley sums up the effectiveness one mother can have on the world: "I learned more about Christianity from my mother than from all the theologians in England."[3]

What if we as women could get a vision for the bigger picture for our kids? What if we viewed our role as a mother as one who could change history? What if we took on the heart of the Lord and stopped pushing away the very thing we are crafted to do?

WITHOUT VISION

Where there is no vision, the people perish (Proverbs 29:18 KJV).

Since, then, you have been raised with Christ, set your hearts on things above, where Christ is, seated at the right hand of God. Set your minds on things above, not on earthly things (Colossians 3:1-2 NIV).

Getting a vision for the immense change in the world you can make by sending out your own missionaries, or arrows from your home, changes the perspective with which we view everything (see Ps. 127:4).

Women today have been told that being a mother is outdated and old-fashioned. They have been sold a lie that they would bring change to the world more effectively by doing something else, and the effects have been catastrophic. The messages told us by society today say to us that having children means missing something. The picture portrayed is one of the grass being greener on the other side, and that if and when we have children, we need to "get them raised" so we can get on with doing something more worthwhile. Although many of us would not say this out loud, we often live this way.

I am not saying we cannot affect the world in other ways—we certainly can and we should. I am simply bringing motherhood up to its rightful place when it comes to changing generations. Being a mother is second only to being a lover of Jesus and a godly wife. It is one of the greatest avenues we have to affect others in many generations to follow. I agree with Elisabeth Elliot's words written to her daughter, "Have no difficulty whatever in saying that my deepest sense of 'fulfillment,' my highest human joys, have been found in being a wife and a mother."[4] The "we can have it all" mindset has left many children to be second place to mommy's higher aspirations. It is not until many women reach their later years of life that they realize that the greatest opportunity they had in life was through being a wife and mother.

The answer to all of this is to understand that our life affects our children and, ultimately, the world. When I really began to see how much more I could change the world through intentionally raising my kids, it motivated me to give it my all.

I remember walking into stores and church services and having other women look at me and say, "Don't worry, it is only a season—you will get through it." At the time I would take encouragement with such a statement. But now when I hear that, I hear it differently—I think, "This is going to pass so fast; before I know it this season will be over. What I am doing with it? Am I enjoying it, and am I investing into this season all my capabilities?" I now actually use that statement to spur me to take full advantage of this time, because I will never get it again. I fear regret more than anything; I want to be able to stand before God and say with full confidence that I did my best and was faithful in what He gave me to steward.

In the early years of raising our children, we were in full-time evangelism, traveling around the world, often moving to various locations for extended periods of time. Whenever we could do this as a family, we would. However, as our family grew in number, the logistics and financial strain of this lifestyle began to become unrealistic for us to maintain. This resulted in Antonio traveling without us an average of two weeks every month for many years.

Antonio would come home from these trips, telling me about all the events that took place during his time away. I listened and remembered when I was there with him, and I began to feel like I was *missing something*. My mind would think back to the spilled milk; piles of laundry; grocery shopping with one child crying, one running away, and another asking to buy everything in sight. I always wanted to have children of my own, but my seemingly unglamorous life at this point consisted of sleepless nights, feedings, messy toddlers, and dirty diapers. I ended each day exhausted, collapsing into bed, only to do it all over again. It certainly did not seem like what I was doing was important. In fact, rarely did anyone ever see me do these things.

It was during this season that the rubber began to meet the road. I needed to find the purpose behind what I was doing. I knew in my heart that this was important, but I needed a transformation in my heart. God had me right where He wanted me. It was in this place that a slow progression of embracing motherhood was working in me. I agree with the book *True Christian Motherhood*, which states:

> I believe there is an uprising movement of mothers who want to find their way back home. God is stirring up the hearts of mothers all around the world to return their hearts back toward their husbands and their children. Trust that this return will not be easy—it will mean being nothing less than countercultural. It will mean doing what the neighbors aren't. It will mean looking different from other moms. It will mean defending your children as a gift from God. It will mean sacrificing everything. Your very ALL...for the next generation. And it will all be worth it—every last breath.[5]

We have adapted a worldview that looks nothing like the way God sees and feels and, therefore, it is not truth. We live and feel this way because the value placed on this calling is so low in our culture; it is commonly considered lesser to the many other things available for us to do. So how can we help not feeling trapped in the house? How can we escape the real feelings of exhaustion we have all experienced, or wanting to be noticed and praised for some skill or ability other than changing a diaper in ten seconds flat?

The answer to this is vision. Without vision we truly do perish because we do not have the understanding of the power we have or the motivation to see the effects of our actions. I know so many women today who are strong, capable, smart, and talented. Yet with all of this wonderful gifting inside of them, they are rarely encouraged to use it to bring up the next generation in an intentional way. To find a role model who truly embraces being a mother today is rare.

To mother effectively, to be a woman like Susanna Wesley and the many others like her, we need vision. Not just any vision, but God's vision. When we get God's vision to become our vision, then we can do our part in fulfilling His purposes on the earth. We need to see our part in God's story.

So what then does God have to say about motherhood? I want to invite you to join me as we explore God's heart for motherhood and how we can partner with Him in making disciples of all nations, one home at a time, starting with our own.

SERVANT OF ALL

It was a cold day in February 2003, when I walked in the front door and crumpled onto the couch. I was tired—very tired. Our first son, Michael, who was now two and a half years old, had a chest cold, and our seven-week-old Gabriel had a double ear infection. They were both cranky, not sleeping—neither was I. They had both fallen asleep in the car and I had managed by some miracle to keep Michael asleep and lay him in his bed, and then I set the sleeping baby in the car seat next to me by the couch. "There," I thought, "finally I can take a nap." I closed my stinging eyes and, just as I began to doze off, I heard crying from the bedroom and a loud, "I'm thirsty." Michael's scream was followed by a crying baby, which was followed by an overtired, now crying mom. "How am I going to do this?" I thought. My dreams of being a mom just seemed to dwindle down to getting a shower. I wanted a big family, but how was I going to have that if I could barely handle two kids? I had always wanted to be a mom, but the formula of no sleep, chronic ear infections, a colicky baby, an active toddler, and cooking and cleaning just felt like too much. I was beginning to wonder what I was doing wrong. Did anyone even care what I was doing? These tasks seemed so insignificant. I wanted to make a difference.

I am sure I had read Colossians 3:23-24 hundreds of times before, but this particular day it hit me like a ton of bricks. God was showing me something, something that changed my perspective forever. Paul said, *"Whatever you do, work at it with all your heart, as working for the Lord, not for human masters, since you know that you will receive an inheritance from the Lord as a reward. It is the Lord Christ you are serving"* (Col. 3:23-24 NIV). There it was. Whatever I do, I was to do it for the Lord. And if I did it with all my heart, I would get an inheritance from Him.

My mind reeled with thoughts of all the things I did in my day that seemed so insignificant. There I sat, knowing that God was speaking to me so clearly that I could do all this unto Him! I felt a new lease on life, and a new meaning behind what I was doing. I could work and serve in my home when no one was looking and know that God saw it all. He saw my heart, my intentions, and now He was inviting me to do all I did for Him as worship. I could move His heart by the way I carried mine.

This revelation started me down a path of joy. I thought continuously about living my life before His eyes and loving Him by being a wife and mom who pursued growth in character. God was showing me that everything has value when I am doing it before the eyes of God. I began to use the Holy Spirit to help me handle situations. I asked Him what He thought about what I was doing.

This revelation grew into not only loving God through loving my family, but I began to get a passion for it. I started to see my home and being a wife and mother as my life's work—it became my ministry. I was raising not only my kids, but I was privileged to have the opportunity to alter the many generations who will follow. If I don't do this, then who will? I studied godly women throughout history and talked to moms who had kids who loved Jesus. I could be the avenue through which revival is unleashed. I realized I could, like Susanna Wesley, Sarah Edwards, and many others before me, change the world for Christ through my home more effectively than any other way. I was anointed for it, equipped, and now I had the vision and grace to make it a reality.

My emotions began to change as my thoughts and purpose changed. When I stopped meditating on how hard it was, stopped saying I couldn't handle certain things, and I started getting God's vision, that transformed me. This transformation in my thinking was in actuality renewing my mind with the Bible, and it was making me a new person. I thought different, which made me feel different, which in turn made me act different. Mothers, we need to recognize that what is done in our homes is work for the Lord! We can change history.

ETERNAL PERSPECTIVE

Do you not know that in a race all the runners run, but only one gets the prize? Run in such a way as to get the prize (1 Corinthians 9:24 NIV).

Do not lay up for yourselves treasures on earth, where moth and rust destroy and where thieves break in and steal; but lay up for yourselves treasures in heaven, where neither moth nor rust destroys and where thieves do not break in and steal. For where your treasure is, there your heart will be also (Matthew 6:19-21).

A grave mistake that we can so easily get caught up in is having a temporal mindset. Having an eternal perspective has vast importance in life, and it should be the thinking we have in everything, especially in how we mother our children. This brings so much joy, purpose, and encouragement to know that we can store up treasures in Heaven through even the tiniest of actions that are unseen by men, but seen by God. If we store up earthly treasure, we will be earthly minded and our heart will be here; but if we store up heavenly treasure, we will be heavenly minded and our heart will be there. We are eternal beings, and every action we do on this side of Heaven directly affects how we will spend eternity.

We have a reward that has been designated for us, and that we have worked for, but we are warned of the possiblity of losing that which we worked so hard to earn: *"Watch out that you do not lose what we have worked for, but that you may be rewarded fully"* (2 John 1:8 NIV). We must live our lives and run our race in such a way as to win the prize. Paul exhorts that we go into "strict training." This is something we must do intentionally as an athlete does, with eternity as our aim. We must begin to think eternally and let our actions come from that place.

Having an eternal perspective means evaluating the beliefs, events, decisions, and actions of life from God's point of view. It is using God's values as the measuring stick with which we evaluate life. Having an eternal perspective is recognizing that everything done in the present has an eternal consequence and should be evaluated in that light. We can view the world through "spiritual eyes," with God's perspective, or we can simply view the world through "physical eyes" and fail to grasp the eternal. Our view of life will greatly affect our thinking and actions, as well as how we live for eternity. Eternal thinking is God's thinking. Eternity is not just something we think about; it is the lens through which we are to view life.

Every decision we make, whether in secret or open, God records and we are rewarded for it. So the good news is that God sees even our good intentions and godly desires. Actions spurred on by a godly value system are what give us treasures in Heaven. We do not have to find our importance or value in the false and temporal value system of what man thinks. We have freedom and joy, knowing that when we give of ourselves, whether it is our time, money, or energy, a glorious and just God sees us. It makes it so easy to work when we are doing it unto God. And it also makes it easier to die and give our very life for Him, because Paul said, *"To live is Christ, and to die is gain"* (Phil. 1:21). Paul also said:

> *Therefore we do not lose heart. Though outwardly we are wasting away, yet inwardly we are being renewed day by day. For our light and momentary troubles are achieving for us an eternal glory that far outweighs them all. So we fix our eyes not on what is seen, but on what is unseen, since what is seen is temporary, but what is unseen is eternal* (2 Corinthians 4:16-18 NIV).

To have an eternal perspective, we must have God's values, and His values are His Word. We must meditate and study these values until they become our own. The Bible is the ultimate truth by which we live and measure our life. Every decision we make for God matters. Do not be dismayed by momentary troubles and trials, for they are working for us a far more exceeding weight of glory.

As we walk out being a mother, the best way to do that is with having a mindset that's eternal, which produces fruit that will last.

A FIRE IN YOUR SPIRIT

That He would grant you, according to the riches of His glory, to be strengthened with might through His Spirit in the inner man (Ephesians 3:16).

To have kids who are on fire for God doesn't just happen. Our kids are a reflection of us in the natural realm, and the same is true of their spiritual condition—it all too often mirrors our spiritual condition. God is raising up a company of women who are not just smart but wise; who value purity, caring more about inner beauty than outer; who live their lives laid down for others, starting with their own family; and who live for the eyes of God. God is looking for those women who are willing to experience the joy of giving and, as a result, getting more than we ever dreamed possible. This has to start with prayer that is birthed out of intimacy with God.

When we are being spiritually lazy, putting more priority on sports, education, and music lessons than our own lives, the spiritual condition of our kids will reflect that. When we ourselves are on fire for Jesus, it can be more easily passed on to our children. In both the negative and the positive sense, our kids reflect us. And mothers, this is crucial for us because we spend more time with our kids than anyone else. We can run our homes, marriages, and families much better with hearts that are alive in God. When we have a spark in our spirit and have regular time with Him, it shows in the way we do life. Our kids will pick up on it. It is so important that we not only make time to be with the Lord, but we make it a priority above all else. We can't afford *not* to. This is not a point for taking on yet another thing we feel we are falling short in. Rather, it is an encouragement to know that when we spend time with God, He multiplies our efforts. He moves things we cannot.

Prayer is an act of humility and dependence that says to God, "I can't do it on my own. I need You." Our lack of prayer, or finding time for it, displays our obvious misunderstanding of its value and necessity. It is pride that says we do not need Him. I have five kids and struggle to find the time to do it all. But I have had many times of prayerlessness and quickly learned that the strength, emotional steadiness, spiritual refreshing, and intimacy I get from those times far outweigh any sacrifice I make to do it. In fact, I backtrack in all areas of my life when I do not spend regular time with God. I can't afford not to pray. I have also learned that there are moments, even in the life of the busy mom, where we can take the time to be with God. It is not as impossible as it seems.

Here are some helpful tips when trying to establish a prayer life as a busy wife and mother. Begin with finding a time to do it. For me, it's usually the morning or sometimes when the kids take a nap. It has varied over the years, depending on the season of life I am in. I soon discover that once I taste God, I get very creative in finding the time because *I want to*. When something is enjoyable, we will find the time to do it. Although having a nap, a pedicure, a massage, or surfing Facebook is fun and relaxing, the refreshment of the spirit will far outweigh the refreshment of the body.

Once you schedule that time, make prayer lists and pray and read the Word. Speak the Bible back to God, asking Him to touch you. There are many great tips in Antonio's book *Relentless Pursuit*, and I encourage you to try every one of them. Soon you will not be able to live without having a set-apart time with God. It is also important to walk with Him all day long. You can pray in tongues in the shower, while folding laundry, or while cooking dinner. I keep a small Bible in my purse and will periodically sing a line of Scripture, pray it, say it, or meditate on it. I do this in the grocery store, on the treadmill, blow-drying my hair, or whatever I find myself doing. It is possible to do all that needs to get done and still have our hearts set on God. It may take some time to establish this in your life, but don't give up! God sees even your desire to be with Him and it moves His heart. He will give you the grace to do it if you will ask Him.

IN-HOME DISCIPLESHIP

John Wesley said, "If I can find ten men who hate nothing but sin, love nothing but God, and seek nothing but the souls of men, we can turn England upside down for God."[6] This rings true and its achievement is most naturally and easily fulfilled in our home with our kids. Where else will we get someone to disciple at such an intimate level, who loves us, looks up to us, and allows us to speak directly into their heart? The opportunity to change the world for Jesus and advance the Kingdom is most readily available within the walls of our homes, but so often we seek it elsewhere and fail to see the opportunity right in front of us.

I want to look for a little bit at what is important and what isn't. Even in being a mom we put different comparisons, pressures, and expectations on ourselves. There is a perfectionism mindset that needs to be dismantled, which can easily derail our efforts by stealing our time. As soon as I had two kids, and eventually five, I began to realize very fast that something had to give. I couldn't keep the house as clean as I wanted and still be the mom I wanted to be. Priorities had to be in place, and I was forced to make daily choices. In fact, I had to weigh my priorities; when I stepped back and asked myself what kind of kids I wanted, it became very clear what my priorities had to be. I did learn how to better manage my time, how to cook healthy meals quickly and keep the house tidy, but my motivation and drive was and is that I want kids who are on fire for Jesus. I want kids who know God for themselves. I want kids who not only know the Bible but also know the God in it. Having children like this doesn't just happen.

Many people assume it's just happenstance to get a child who follows God's ways, but I assure you it is very dependent on how that child was raised. Yes, kids do make their own decisions, but they draw from the pool of what's been instilled in them. It is up to us as parents to sow the seeds that will produce the right fruit in time; it is not the job of the Sunday school, the teacher, or anyone else—it is up to us. And it is also up to us to make sure that other seeds that would choke out the good seeds are not sown into their lives. We are to guard everything—what they watch, what they listen to, and what friends they have. All of their influence comes under our evaluation in light of God's Word, teaching them to do the same thing.

We as parents are their covering, and it's our God-given responsibility to see that we steward our children in a way that honors Him. We simply cannot afford to give away our spiritual authority to our children and let them "make their own decisions." We are going to stand before the Lord and give account for how we handled them. This is not to say that we are to be overbearing and dictate our child's every action. But it does mean we guide them in all things, say no to many things, and not allow anything that opposes God or His Word. Spiritual things and obedience to God and the Bible are of upmost importance.

BIBLICAL WORLDVIEW

If we instill a biblical worldview in them from an early age, they will not only understand our stance on issues, but they will make them their own. Many Christian kids walk away from God in their early adult years because they have a nonbiblical worldview. They have been given rules without being taught the biblical reasons why those rules exist. In other words, they have a mix of the world's ways and God's, and the world's ways are choking out the truth. We have to be vigilant in raising our kids without "the mixture" of the world.

What is sown in their hearts is what will grow and produce fruit in their lives. When they are released from our covering, the worldview they have will be what comes out of their hearts. It is very important that they don't have only guidelines from us, but that they also have the reasons why. They will own what you're instructing them if they see the importance of it and have a reverence for God, as well as intimacy with Him for themselves. It is vital to instill all we can from the earliest possible age and trust God to do the rest.

There is value and an incredible glory in being a mother, which you were created for. You affect the Kingdom and get to write on the pages of history. You can raise kids who are equipped to live a life of radical obedience to the Lord in a culture that opposes it. As a mother, begin to embrace it—you are producing fruit that will last.

Chapter 7

AIMING YOUR ARROWS

*Behold, children are a heritage from the Lord, the fruit
of the womb is a reward. Like arrows in the hand of a
warrior, so are the children of one's youth. Happy is the
man who has his quiver full of them; they shall not be
ashamed, but shall speak with their enemies in the gate.*

—PSALM 127:3-5

When we raise up children, we are raising up arrows in the
hand of the Lord. In other words, we are fashioning our
children to be ammunition against the works of the enemy.
Arrows are meant to be sharp, deadly, and accurate. We see
from Psalm 127:3-5 that we as parents have a responsibility to
make sure our kids are ready to contend with their enemies.
This job is not for the church to do; instead, the job of forming
godly character and a biblical worldview starts and stops with
the parents.

Unquestionably, we all want children who can and are ready to
face the world and fight well for the Kingdom of God. We all want
children who are equipped, prepared, and ready to be influencers,

not the influenced. We dream of their greatness and success from the moment they are born. We dream that they would go further, harder, and stronger than us.

The real question is then, *How do we prepare our kids to live after God for the long haul? How can we raise children who contend with their enemies, fight their adversaries, and are victorious?*

HOUSTON, WE HAVE A PROBLEM

In the book *Family Driven Faith*, Voddie Baucham, Jr. says:

> The church in America is in trouble. Teens are abandoning the faith in astounding numbers. Birth rates are plummeting as our attitude toward children continues to sour. The overwhelming majority of those who call themselves Christians do not think biblically, and the answer given most often is better youth ministry. In case you don't think this is a major issue, consider the following statistics. With a birth rate hovering around two children per family, a biblical worldview rate below 10 percent, and about 75 percent of our teens leaving the church by the end of their freshman year in college, it currently takes two Christian families in one generation to get a single Christian into the next generation. "Houston, we have a problem."[1]

We want to encourage you that no matter how bad things are, you can break any negative cycle for your home and the generations that follow. God has given us His Word and clear direction on how to raise our children, and we simply must get back to the ancient paths. Christian families are losing their children by the masses, and we must fight because the stakes are high.

THINGS THAT DERAIL

Knowing what to do in raising kids on fire for God is imperative, but in doing the right things we cannot let sin and compromise come in and derail all that we are instilling into our children. We have seen many godly couples make some mistakes, the effects of which were astronomical to the spiritual well-being of their kids.

One of the most common mistakes is giving away your spiritual authority to your kids. Parents who do this often have a stronger value on "friendship style" parenting than they do on making sure their kids know right and wrong. This parent works more to be a friend than a parent. Although our kids are and will be some of our greatest friends in life, while raising them our focus is to train them in the ways of God, not to be their best friend. We will give an account before the Lord as to how well we did that in this life.

Our children will have many friends, but only one set of parents, so we must take our job seriously. You, as their parent, are responsible for everything—what they watch, hear, see, and whom they spend time with—and, ultimately, you are the controller of what is influencing their life. Many godly families have allowed other influences into their homes simply by the passivity of being a friend before a parent. This must stop. Our kids are depending on us to lead them on the right paths; therefore, we can *not* let go of the reins for them to choose for themselves what is right and what is wrong. Whether your kids like it or not, understand it or not, it is you who will answer to God for how well you parented them.

We don't give our kids final say over where they can attend school, the movies they get to watch, or the music they listen to. They can have input within the parameters we have set for them, but there should be no further choices beyond the options we give. When given the wise options and the understanding of why these options are allowed, we have found they do not feel as though they are missing out on anything. When we speak to our kids about the dangers of certain choices, we have found that not only do they just obey, but they do it willingly and eventually on their own. It is our privilege to guide them and give them clear instruction and discipleship for life.

We have had many parents say to us that they don't want to push their kids away or drive them to rebellion, or that they want them to learn to make their own decisions. Our kids know the values and standards expected of them from a very young age; they know full well that we will make sure they will have knowledge of God's ways to the best of our ability, not just *what* to do but *why* they are to do it. Their life depends on making the Bible their guidebook for life and living. As long as our kids are under our care, God's ways are the only ways that we will allow in our home. Our children understand that we work to demonstrate to them that we ultimately answer to God for their lives.

Compromise and lethargy can come in slowly through making the world's ways our worldviews until we think they are normal. What we do both positively and negatively as parents in our personal life directly affects our kids. They will do what we do, not necessarily what we say. We must work to demonstrate what a life after God looks like, and show them how to live that way too. And when we fail, we repent, make it right, and start over again. This demonstrates to them a pattern for how to live their life.

There have been countless times when we have failed and had to humble ourselves before our children. I (Antonio) remember one time that Christelle and I got in a very heated "discussion." Any couple knows what I'm talking about. Anyway, one of the rules that we have for fighting in our marriage is to never fight in front of the kids. Well, my emotions got the better of me, and we fought in front of the kids. After I came to my senses, I sat all of the kids down in our living room and told them that what took place was wrong. I asked them to forgive me. It was a great opportunity to show them through my own mistakes how to repent before God and before family.

Typically, compromise comes in when parents do not hold the line in the areas of music, movies, friends, family, and school. Christian parents have been lulled to sleep while the enemy comes to destroy their kids right in front of them. We have the ability to control the stream of influence that flows into their lives in a huge measure, and we must use it. It is a great privilege and responsibility.

BAD COMPANY CORRUPTS

Do not be misled: "Bad company corrupts good character" (1 Corinthians 15:33 NIV).

Even a child is known by his deeds, whether what he does is pure and right (Proverbs 20:11).

We can train up our children in a way that their character is formed to be godly, yet if we allow the bad company of certain friendships, then that can come in and corrupt our children. The friends we allow around our children must be strategic and guarded, for they will be a voice into their lives, and they will either strengthen or destroy the character being developed. This is not an area to take lightly, and it must be a point of open, honest conversation with your kids. They must learn to regularly and correctly evaluate their peers and learn to discern who walks with God and who does not by the fruit those friends produce.

Our kids are like wet cement, and we have to guard what is imprinted upon them. We discuss with our kids regularly about the behaviors and choices others around them are making. We refuse to allow our children to have deep friendships with other children who are not pursuing the ways of God. This is not legalism, but wisdom. Psalm 1:1-2 speaks about this when it says:

> *Blessed is the one who does not walk in step with the*
> *wicked or stand in the way that sinners take or sit in*
> *the company of mockers, but whose delight is in the*
> *law of the Lord, and who meditates on his law day*
> *and night* (NIV).

This verse shows the progression of walking with wickedness that leads to standing in the ways of sinners, which eventually leads to sitting purposefully in rebellion against God. Our kids, over time and through training, have to recognize for themselves this progression and the dangers of bad company corrupting them. They are growing in wisdom as they learn to recognize the evidences of God in a person's life and how to carefully choose their friendships with our guidance.

One particular time we began to notice lifestyle choices of a certain friend of one of our sons and observed the destructive path he was headed down. After having this brought to our attention, we talked to our son and discussed with him what we saw in his friend and why we were not going to let him spend time with him outside of what was necessary for school and sports functions. He did not fight us or beg us for another verdict, but instead he cried with sadness at the realization of where his friend was with God. We were able to sit with our son and pray for his friend together. Although we prayed for him, the friendship with that young man came to a halt, and the decision helped set up our son for future decisions that were similar, which he made on his own as the years progressed.

This has happened many times since then with all of our children. They know clearly that although we show love and kindness and share Jesus and pray for those around us, we do not give ourselves to be influenced by anyone or anything that contradicts God's ways and whose life does not have evidence of hunger for God. While our kids are in our care, they are being shaped and fashioned, and are not yet ready to be on their own as *missionaries* in hostile anti-God environments where they are easily influenced. We must protect them and make sure that what's imprinted on them is what we want to last. They can be corrupted, as no person is exempt to this principle.

Bad company can also come in the form of music. It is very common to see young children listening to secular pop artists whose music and lives promote sexual promiscuity, rebellion against parents, and whose lyrics and actions are brainwashing the minds of our kids. Part of the problem is that many parents are also being discipled by these artists, and, as a result, fail to see the problem with it. Any amount of poison is deadly, and much of this content and attitude is extremely deadly to our souls. We must be alert, be of sober mind, and be watchful, for the enemy is prowling around like a lion, seeking to devour our kids any way he can (see 1 Pet. 5:8). We have to be spiritually violent in our mission as parents to stand for truth and purity, and to have a life and home of no compromise. Most of the pre-teen and teen culture out there that comes forth through music is showing our kids how to live a life of compromise. It is not "cute," and we must not put up with it. It cannot be treated lightly or innocently; we are to have a "no tolerance" policy for immorality or sin of any kind. Our kids will act and reflect what and who influences them.

Television is another obvious avenue that secular mindsets can become instilled in our children. To say that TV has influence on our children is a gross understatement. Voddie Baucham, Jr. states:

> I can't tell you how many times my wife and I have been told that we are stifling our children because they are only allowed to watch four hours of television per week (the national average has been stated as four and a half to five hours per day) or because my fifteen-year-old daughter is not allowed to date. Inevitably we hear the standard cop-out argument, "When they get to college, they're going to go crazy!" Interestingly, though, none of the "wild ones" I remember from my college days were rookies. None of them went off the deep end into immorality after leading chaste lives at home. Most of them simply walked farther into the debauchery with which they were allowed to experiment earlier on.[2]

It is not extreme to keep from our children influences that will corrupt them; as a matter of fact, it is love and they will thank us for it. They are far too young to make these decisions for themselves, and we as parents must hold the line and the standard of righteousness in our homes.

We have found, in our attempts at having a God-centered home with boundaries and consequences, that it has created for our kids a place of safety. They know and appreciate what we have set out to do; they feel safe and have a greater sense of freedom within those boundaries. There is no easy way or shortcut to this. Holding the line comes with continuously standing for righteousness, explaining to our kids the *why* behind the *what* we are expecting of them. It is a life of sharing Scripture, using real-life opportunities to explain biblical truths, being there with love and correction when they fail, and encouraging and guiding them every step of the way. It is a lifestyle that is not for the faint of heart, but its rewards are well worth it.

BIBLICAL WORLDVIEW

When addressing how to raise kids who follow after God, we look at areas where the norms of the culture have outplayed biblical truth. Just because society says that something is normal doesn't make it biblical or normal according to God's perspective. The ultimate goal for raising our children should be that they have a biblical worldview. Whatever worldview any of us possess dictates how we live life—it is the way we see life. We must see life through the lens of the Bible and line our lives up to it in every way.

If we can succeed as parents with giving our kids a biblical worldview, the chances of them walking away from their faith when they are older diminish greatly. We must be a people without a mixture of cultural norms and God's ways; we must reject cultural norms that contradict the Bible. George Barna discovered that 85 percent of Christian teens do not believe in the existence of absolute truth.[3] But we would argue, to not believe in absolutes is to not be a Christian—God's Word is absolute truth. This sad statistic shows the failure with which Christian kids are being raised and matches closely to the statistics of young people leaving the faith by their first year of college. This is not a coincidence.

REWARD FROM HIM, HERITAGE FROM THE LORD

Children are a heritage from the Lord, offspring a reward from him (Psalm 127:3 NIV).

Having children is a heritage from the Lord. We are happy and blessed when we have children, because God is actually giving them to us as a reward that comes directly from Him. This does not mean that those who cannot have children have been judged by the Lord in any way; only that children come *from Him*. It is important to not read into that too much. It is our experience that those who do not have physical children are very much involved in fathering and mothering in many different ways. We will discuss the great need for fathers and mothers further in other chapters, but this too has great worth in the sight of God, as many are searching and desiring spiritual fathering and mothering.

When you read the Bible, it doesn't take long to see that from God's standpoint children are given to us to strengthen, influence, be a blessing, and so much more. God equates children to wealth and power. As a matter of fact, when you read through the Old Testament you will often see that when God blessed people, it was through giving them children and physical wealth, such as livestock, often both being in the same sentence. In Matthew we see how Jesus welcomes little children: *"Whoever welcomes one such child in my name welcomes me"* (Matt. 18:5 NIV). He doesn't see them as an inconvenience, burdensome, and to be overlooked until they reach a certain age or maturity level. Children are the next generation of world changers, and they will carry a greater load and responsibility than we are in our own generation. As darkness is ever increasing, it is more important than ever that we shake off the sin that so easily entangles us and run the race set out before us (see Heb. 12:1). Part of our race is our responsibility to shape and disciple those younger than us in the ways of God. To build an empire we must first build a family.

AIMING OUR ARROWS

Arrows are weapons meant to be pointed toward something. It is one of our main jobs as parents to aim our kids toward a mark, and even to shoot them at it. We have to be intentional about training them up in the way they should go, so that when they are older they will hit the mark that they have been aimed at (see Prov. 22:6).

Too many parents are playing a defensive role when it comes to parenting. They hope their kids won't drink, smoke, sleep around, or do drugs; instead, we must take an offensive parenting method, which is to raise and train our kids to love God with their all hearts. Many people say to us, "You are blessed to have such great kids." We know they are implying that we are just lucky to have all of our kids walking with God. Although we do have great kids and are blessed, we can assure you that it is no accident that they are walking with the Lord. In fact, anyone who desires to train up their children in the ways of God can have it. It is nothing short of a lot of hard work, prayer, and with great intention that we are seeing our children grow up knowing God and walking in His ways. It is not easy raising kids in today's culture, and it takes great spiritual violence to stay true to the ancient paths of God's Word and instill it in them at every possible chance.

Another thing many parents do is make their dreams for their children too small. We hope they marry a good person, get a decent job, and move out of the house. But our main dream and aim should be to have children who know God, know how to talk with Him, hear from Him, and have a solid foundation in the Word of God. These kinds of children are unstoppable and have a limitless future of a life full of the dreams of God. But to get children on fire for God won't just happen by accident—we must be deliberate and sharpen our arrows, refining them carefully in the things of God.

This should be our dream, aim, and ultimate parenting goal, far exceeding education, sports, or anything else in this life.

OLDER GENERATIONS

Personally, many times through the years we have made it a point of getting together with various older, more seasoned couples who have grown kids, and learning all we can from their victories and defeats. The combination of doing this with the wisdom of the Holy Spirit, much prayer, and diligence has helped us parent our children to this point in each of their lives. And although we have many years of parenting left, we wanted to share with you some of what we learned so far. Moses reminded the children of Israel:

> *Only be careful, and watch yourselves closely so that you do not forget the things your eyes have seen or let them fade from your heart as long as you live. Teach them to your children and to their children after them* (Deuteronomy 4:9 NIV).

And again:

> *Teach them to your children, talking about them when you sit at home and when you walk along the road, when you lie down and when you get up* (Deuteronomy 11:19 NIV).

In these two verses, we see that we were intended to have the Lord always before us, to have His wonderful deeds and instructions be talked about regularly—when we walk, talk, sit, rise, and sleep. The idea is that we must, at any chance possible, teach the ways of the Lord to our children and even our grandchildren.

Here are a few practical ways we do this as family, and we hope that you use these as a starting point that spurs on more God ideas and opportunities for you and your family:

- **Make family traditions around teaching the Bible:** One way we do this is every Saturday morning we have family breakfast time together. We use this time to laugh and talk and touch on issues of the week or maybe something that is stirring in our hearts from the Lord. Antonio will begin to teach our family on a certain Scripture or principle. If nothing arises spontaneously, we will finish up breakfast and then go to the living room and open our Bibles. Antonio leads this, and it has proved to be a very powerful time where the kids learn immensely and our family is strengthened. If you do not know where to start, you can just begin in Genesis and read. You study and glean from the Word and teach them what you are learning. Many of our ministry teachings were practiced teaching them to our family first.

- **Make the Bible, prayer, and worship a priority:** One of the simplest ways we do this is by having worship on in our home nearly 24/7. We keep our living room our prayer room. This creates an atmosphere in our home that is focused on the presence of God. Another thing we do is take time whenever we can at night and pray in tongues as a family. We often end the night with rallying everyone up and having them do what we call "tongue time" (praying in tongues). The kids love it. We also do this when we are in the car and at other spontaneous moments. The Holy

Spirit will often give us phrases to pray during this time, and sometimes it leads to us praying over each other, prophesying, declaring, and worshiping God.

- **Train our kids to spend time with God on their own:** We try our best to give our kids every opportunity possible to encounter God for themselves. When you taste Him and see Him, you just want more of Him. We have found that the more they get into His presence and hear His voice, the less we have to encourage them to have times with God. However, we do have them set a schedule to be with God regularly and work to maintain it.

- **Take daily opportunities:** We can use daily opportunities life brings to teach them biblical principles, Scripture, and how to integrate it into normal life. We can do this in the car, grocery store, neighborhood, or really anywhere. Driving can be a great time to talk and share your heart with your kids and hear theirs. Listen to them and teach them—use the conversations about normal daily things to teach life lessons they will never forget. Kids learn much from watching us, so how we act, respond, and live will be imitated. We often say that kids do half of our good and double our bad. So what we do is much more important than what we say. Gone are the days when we only tell our kids how to live; we also need to show them how to live with our lives. We teach by doing and by instructing. We even use our own shortcomings as opportunities to teach our kids— and they respect us for it.

- **Get your kids around people on fire for God:** We work hard to teach our kids to encounter and know God, as well as know about Him. One big mistake we have seen and made in the past is to focus all of our time on teaching kids about God through Bible lessons, memorization, and memorized prayers. We still do this, and it is very important, but they can miss knowing Him as they are taught *about* Him. When we introduced our kids to God, we introduced them to the Holy Spirit, Jesus, and the Father. We introduced them to a real God they can interact with on many levels.

The first thing we do after they give their lives to the Lord is teach them how to hear God's voice for themselves. They all picked it up so fast, it was startling. We created the atmosphere, welcomed the Holy Spirit, and told them to ask one question to God, "What do You think about me?" They did this and God spoke to them clearly and directly. They had no doubt in their minds that God was real, and that simple act started them down a path of knowing Him for themselves.

So we highly encourage teaching kids this model of *simple prophecy* from the start, asking God what He thinks about them and others. We also teach them the Word, have them memorize and pray and read the Word out loud. They can know right from the start how to dialogue with God while reading the Word. Kids do not have a junior Holy Spirit—they have the real deal, so introduce your kids to Him.

SETTING YOUR KIDS UP FOR ENCOUNTER

Although we have already touched on many things that will help your kids encounter God, we can't stress enough the importance of encounter. The answer for your kids, no matter their age, is nothing more than God Himself. Knowing Him, receiving His revelation, hearing His voice, and experiencing His weighty presence is what forever transforms. No person, whether a child or an adult, can walk away unchanged when having encountered the living God.

Sometimes being busy with the many things of life can rob our kids of the encounters available for them. Ballet, soccer, church activities, school activities, volunteering, and even serving are some examples of what is vying for their attention. There is certainly nothing wrong with extracurricular activities and doing all of these things, but we must guard our time and social activities carefully so we leave margins for encountering God.

Jesus demonstrates this truth while in the home of Mary and Martha. Martha was busy working, and Mary was sitting at Jesus's feet listening to Him and being with Him. As Martha worked, she became frustrated, and, in the midst of her frustration with Mary's perceived laziness, Jesus wisely says, *"One thing is needed, and Mary has chosen that good part"* (Luke 10:42). Jesus understood that amidst the endless stream of things that keep us busy, the real need is only met through spending time with Him.

Let's never forget what we were made for—Him. He is our satisfaction, our source, our desire, our place of refuge, our safety, and our God in whom we trust. Give your child the gift of encountering God and they will never be the same again.

Chapter 8

DATING GOD'S WAY

As I see it, dating is a product of our entertainment-driven, disposable-everything American culture.
—JOSHUA HARRIS, *I Kissed Dating Goodbye**

It was a hot summer day in 1995, and there we sat on the couch in Antonio's parents' house. We were young, in love, and had no idea what we were doing. But we didn't care. All that seemed to matter in the world was looking into each other's eyes while talking and dreaming about the limitless future that lay ahead of us.

Yet this particular day was different from every other day. This was the day when our parents would go out as couples to discuss how our relationship was going. This day, which took place each month, had quickly become our least favorite. There we would sit freaking out, waiting for our parents to arrive from what had now become regular outings. We couldn't help but wonder what it was they were talking about. We would speculate about what they could be saying, while Antonio's siblings would make knowing smirks and teasing smiles, loving every minute of our "wait" to see if our relationship was going "well" or not.

We were both blessed to grow up in godly families, and, surprisingly, we had parents who had very similar values when it came to relationships. They both decided that we were going to do this God's way, and they were not going to allow anything less. They made that very clear to us from the beginning. They had a biblical understanding of being our "covering," and words cannot express how grateful we are to this day for their leadership in our life. Their covering was preemptive and saved us in so many ways. Although neither of our parents were perfect, they did demonstrate through their care, covering, and sometimes aggressive intervention that they were serious about being parents and showing tough love to us in this tender and crucial season of our lives. Because of their stance and involvement, we knew what was right and wrong. In them we also had someone older and wiser who could see our blind spots and do what was needed to aid our decisions when the "fog" of young love clouded our judgment.

COVERING AND COURTSHIP

Although neither the word *dating* nor *courting* is used in the Bible, for the sake of teaching we are going to use the word *courting* to introduce some God-given concepts and intentions for pre-marriage relationships. Although there is really not a title given for this season of life in the Bible, there is much to say within its pages of how to honor, love, be faithful, be pure, and prepare for all that being married will bring.

The following pages are meant to be a guide to help you maneuver through singleness and dating. Our views on this subject have sadly, in many ways, been tainted and skewed by the world's system of doing things, and, as a result, we are often sabotaged before we even start. It is important we are all on the same page when it comes to how to do things God's way in every season of life.

We have taught on marriage, singleness, raising children, and more. And we have found that only those in that particular season of life come to listen to what is relevant to them—*right now*. However, we encourage you to work to align all of your values with God's in each of these areas regardless of what season you are in at this moment. That way when you, your kids, grandkids, or friends enter into a time where you or they need godly perspective, you will be able to give it.

As we discussed earlier, there has been an idea in our culture that says there is a magical age where a child becomes an adult and therefore no longer needs parental covering. We have taken our cues from society and have often backed off from covering our children just because we are told that they are now an adult. But where in the Bible does going to university or being able to vote or drink alcohol eliminate you or your children from being under a covering? This idea is completely unbiblical, and it is a formula for a long road of bad choices, pain, and excessive emotional baggage.

The argument is that a young adult should make his or her own decisions in order to grow, make mistakes, and learn from them. When we as parents do not cover, however, we relinquish our God-given authority. Now don't get us wrong here; we understand that as children get older they increase in responsibilities, learn to make right choices, and our role as a parent undergoes changes and shifts. But we believe from Scripture that this parental role we are to have is meant to be a covering and a protection for our children all the way until the day they marry, until they leave their father and mother and join to their spouse.

The Bible says, *"Therefore a man shall leave his father and mother and be joined to his wife, and they shall become one flesh"* (Gen. 2:24). There is no in-between adolescent period indicated in this passage that should occur without a covering. This covering we bring to our kids is not meant to be that of an authoritarian dictator, but one of a loving parent who fights for them against the attacks of the enemy. In the same way that husbands are to cover their wives and families, parents are meant to cover their children with a shield of godly counsel, protection, and wisdom.

FIND A COVERING

For those of you reading this who are single, we highly encourage you, no matter how old you are, to find a covering. Ideally, it should be your parents. If it can't be your parents for whatever reason, look for a godly couple and ask them to mentor you and be a father and mother figure in your life. This is a way for you to bring increased security and wisdom to your life, and it can only serve to strengthen you. Allow this couple free reign to speak into areas of sin, weakness, and vulnerability. Also, if your desire is to marry someday, ask them to act as a protection for you as you wait for that godly person to come into your life. Allow them to speak into any potential relationships with open ears, knowing they will see things you do not.

For those of you who have parents willing to speak into your life with godly perspective, embrace that and use whatever they say to bring wisdom and strengthen your future marriage. Give your parents or godly mentors the right to veto any relationship. As believers, we are called to be children of the light and to walk in the light (see 1 Thess. 5:5). And having godly input into our dating relationships, where there's accountability and counsel, provides a strong foundation and produces relationships that are above reproach and that will go for the long haul.

SAVING A MARRIAGE BEFORE IT STARTS

We have five children, two of whom are now teenagers. We are aware that we have many years of parenting to go, and we know already that it's not going to be easy. But from a very young age, we have had regular discussions with our children of our responsibility for them and how we will handle their relationships with the opposite sex. Our job has been to instill in them, to the best of our ability, a biblical worldview regardless of what the culture says is normal.

When a child grows up, whatever worldview they have carried along with them is what is going to come to the surface. For example, when it comes time to choose a mate, they will instinctively act in the way they think is "normal." If they have been taught that they shouldn't court anyone without intent for marriage, this will be their idea of normal as they think about entering a relationship with the opposite sex. In our family, we have made it clear to our children that we will not allow casual "dating" relationships without serious and sober intentions for an eventual lifetime marital commitment.

People have asked us what age we feel is appropriate for dating. The answer is that if your child (or you) is not ready for marriage, there should be no dating—period. Dating without intentions for marriage is just playing irresponsibly with another person's heart, which is dangerous and detrimental. We do not wait to have these talks with our children until they are "old enough" according to the culture. Instead, we make it a part of daily life conversations. Our discussions with our kids are about what kind of person they want to marry and what people around them have those virtues. We teach them to recognize godly character traits and make that their aim in seeking a spouse. What qualities do you want in him or her? What qualities should you possess to be a man or woman of character?

You attract who you are, not who you want. So we can see how imperative it is that everyone gets on the same page about these issues so we can save marriages before they even start. It is vitally important to create their "normal" to be God's way.

DATING CULTURE OF TODAY

Too often the way we do dating in our culture today is with a disposable mindset. Even in Christian circles, the only guidelines given are "don't have sex" and "marry a Christian." People view singleness as merely their time to romantically "try out" guys and girls, with often no real intent of marrying any of them.

We believe that the decline of a culture is marked by its decline in respect for marriage. The way dating is done today lacks respect for marriage in a big way. Our culture is bombarded with humanistic and feminist ideas through education, movies, music, magazines, and even some churches. We are taught to serve self and do what brings us gratification and temporal happiness. These ideas are anti-biblical, anti-God, and against honoring of parents, yet we as a church have bought into them.

People spend so much time planning their wedding day, but not developing their character. We are meant to be a people of character and righteousness who stand out from the world, but sadly the rates of fornication, adultery, divorce, and immorality of all kinds in the church mirror that of the world. Something must be done about this. Marriage is viewed as a contract that we can be freed from as soon as the winds of romance change or our happiness is in jeopardy.

This disposable marriage idea all starts with the disposable dating of our day. We tire of one person, and they don't make us happy, so we move on to the next person. And, sadly, all too often the cycle continues right into our marriages. We minimize the value of our physical bodies by experiencing someone who does not rightfully belong to us. This was never meant to be. We were meant to take the many principles of the Bible and apply them to every area of life, our romantic life included.

RESURGENCE OF HONOR

When we think about the subject of honor according to the Bible, we must recognize that one way we honor God is by honoring those in authority over us. God will honor those who honor Him. We must realize that when our hearts are determined to honor God, He sees that and the honor we give Him produces a great reward. We must seek to have a heart that honors God above all things, and seek to find what actions bring honor to Him in all areas of our life, especially in the pursuit of a spouse.

When we honor others, especially those in authority over us, it turns God toward us. It commands a blessing according to the promises of Scripture: *"'Honor your father and mother,' which is the first commandment with promise: 'that it may be well with you and you may live long on the earth'"* (Eph. 6:2-3). We talked about honoring parents earlier, but we must mention it again here as it is absolutely crucial to have a heart of honor in our relationships both with our parents and our future spouse. Find a way to get parents involved whenever possible and value their input, especially if they are godly people. And if it is not possible to have this, find a couple who can give insight and godly wisdom so you are not alone.

> *But among you there must not be even a hint of sexual immorality, or of any kind of impurity, or of greed, because these are improper for God's holy people* (Ephesians 5:3 NIV).

Another aspect of honor in courting relationships is honoring our bodies and emotions, as well as the body and emotions of another. We should not even consider getting romantically involved in any way with anyone unless it is for the purpose of marriage. This is not only true emotionally but also physically. Have you ever considered that the other person could be someone else's spouse someday? You wouldn't come near a married person, or at least you shouldn't, so you should consider this when looking at a person of the opposite sex.

If a strong parental covering is in place, there will be protection and a safety net that will be beneficial for generations. After all, our children are in our care for protecting, helping, nurturing, and maturing. All of these responsibilities are highly important. Paul reminds us:

> *Flee sexual immorality. Every sin that a man does is outside the body, but he who commits sexual immorality sins against his own body. Or do you not know that your body is the temple of the Holy Spirit who is in you, whom you have from God, and you are not your own? For you were bought at a price; therefore glorify God in your body and in your spirit, which are God's* (1 Corinthians 6:18-20).

We see at the end of this verse that we honor God with our bodies—our body is not our own any longer once we give our lives over to Jesus Christ. Knowing this brings both the fear of the Lord as well as great hope and excitement. We are His! And because we are His, He gives us the power and ability to walk this commandment out. He comes in with His grace (empowerment) upon our *yes* to Him. We must war to be a people without even a hint or a trace of sexual immorality in our lives.

In a society that is laced with sexual immorality and dripping with the seduction and lusts of the flesh, we must make a decision to walk purely. Purity is within the grasp of all who want it by the grace of God. We must be a people without mixture. As darkness increases all around us, we must live in such a way that is set apart in holiness unto the Lord. We do not just separate ourselves from sin, although this is important, but we set ourselves toward Him by turning to Him with our whole heart. No matter what your past, you can start fresh today! Call sin as sin, repent, and turn from sexual immorality. Honor God, yourself, and your future spouse with your body.

WHOLENESS IN SINGLENESS

We have heard the funniest things when it comes to finding that "perfect one." Society, movies, and songs give this message over and over again, that we could possibly miss our "soul mate" if we don't look hard enough. This mindset gives a feeling of desperation. Finding our life mate should not be one of desperation, but rather one of patiently looking for someone with whom we can share God's love and live out God's purposes.

The Bible never suggests there is one right choice for marriage. Rather, all the teaching passages seem to suggest that there are wise and unwise choices. We are encouraged to use wisdom, not fate, as our guide when choosing a marital partner. Once we are married, we have "the one" and that is how God sees it.

Proverbs reminds us, *"A wife of noble character who can find?"* (Prov. 31:10 NIV). This is a perfect verse for men. We should assume as this verse implies that we are to be in a serious pursuit, actively engaging to make a wise choice. The Bible tells young men to search for a woman of character; it reminds these men that while looks won't last, godly character improves with age: *"Charm is deceitful and beauty is passing, but a woman who fears the Lord, she shall be praised"* (Prov. 31:30). It says nothing—absolutely nothing—about "feelings." This verse makes a woman's faith the defining characteristic of her suitability to be an excellent wife.

This is not to say that we are not to find someone who is physically compatible. Simply, however, that the first priority, according to Scripture, is to find a spiritually compatible person, and then, under that umbrella, find a physically attractive person. Not the other way around.

WHAT YOU ARE IS WHAT YOU WILL ATTRACT

Many young people have created a list of what they are looking for in their future spouse. Even though having a vision of what you're looking to find one day is good and should be done, it is more important to realize that who you are and what you stand for today is the type of person you will attract. The reflection of who you are is what you will gravitate toward and who will be attracted to you.

This is not speaking about opposite personalities attracting one another. We are talking about the character, beliefs, and values that you hold dear; these will be what you will attract to yourself. If your views are liberal in nature, expect to attract that type of person. If you value a good-looking guy rather than him being able to provide for you, then you will attract a man who can't hold a job. If you value a girl who says she's a Christian but does not believe in what she says, then that is whom you will attract. You will not attract that which you are not. The focus should be on building *you* and your character.

PRE-MARRIAGE EXPECTATIONS

Singleness is a state that should be pursued and not avoided. It is usually defined as being without a partner, but the real meaning is to be separate, unique, and whole. A single person is complete, not divided or disjointed, but one unit, whole. Another word for whole is *peace*—nothing missing and nothing broken. If you are whole, then that means you're looking for someone who is also whole. You're not looking for another half—not someone who is wounded but healed. The goal is to find another whole person, not a half of a person to complete you.

God wants to satisfy the deep longings of a person's heart. A spouse does fill in the gap as someone for friendship, enjoying life, helping, supporting, encouraging, and companionship. But despite how great a person is, they will never fulfill you. God is your only hope for true fulfillment. He created you to only be truly satisfied in a relationship with Him.

As soon as we put expectations on the other person to be our source of fulfillment, we are in a form of dysfunction. We will eventually get disappointed without exception. Our relationships can contribute to our worth and our fulfillment, but they can never be our source.

Many couples enter into marriage with high expectations, and within weeks or months these expectations are let down, causing many marriages to go into a spiral of dysfunction. When these expectations are not met, it leads to disappointment and distance between each other. It is very important that, even during times of singleness, our expectations are not built on a fantasy or a false view of fulfillment. It is also important when we do marry that we share our expectations with our spouse. They will not know if we do not tell them. Discussing these expectations can lead to healthy conversation and take care of potential disappointment before it ever happens.

FOUR STAGES OF FRIENDSHIP

There are several books out there that help give practical advice on this topic. One book we would recommend to help maneuver through the singleness and courting phase is *I Kissed Dating Goodbye* by Joshua Harris. In his book he states, "Instead of waiting until friendship fully blooms, we rush into romance. Our impatience not only costs us the beauty of friendship as singles; it can also place our future marriages on shaky ground. Strong marriages are built on a solid foundation of the mutual respect, appreciation, and camaraderie of friendship."[1]

Getting too close too soon costs us pieces of our heart, valuable time, and emotional investment that were never meant for any person other than our spouse. Although difficult, growing in friendship allows for us to see a person as they really are without the plastic veneer that typical dating often brings. The person no longer becomes a conquest, but a heart to win and take care of forever. Instead of being selfish in nature, it is serving and giving, looking out for the needs of the other. And when the time comes, it is the job of the man to lead and approach the girl or those who cover her. He must declare his intentions for marriage and that he would like the opportunity to win her heart and her trust. He must also humbly submit to be tested and tried by those who care for and look out for her.

In order to maneuver through a successful, God-focused pre-marital relationship, Joshua Harris gives some advice to describe the five stages of relationships that we find to be a very practical and an insightful way to move forward. These stages are:

1. Casual friendship

2. Deeper friendship

3. Courtship

4. Purposeful intimacy with integrity

5. Engagement[2]

It was not long ago that our society valued commitment, honor, and putting another's needs above our own. Today, however, what we mostly see is dating used as a romantic sport. What used to be something of great value and care is now nothing more than having a good time on a Friday night. The book *From Front Porch to Backseat* documents these changes: "Intimacy didn't have to be accompanied by deepening obligation or responsibility to another person. Love and romance became things people could enjoy solely for their recreational value."[3]

PRINCIPLES OF DATING GOD'S WAY

Our ministry has created a five-month training program called the Pursuit Internship. Ninety-five percent of those who attend are single and in their early 20s. During the last couple of years, in the middle of the training, we have taken one night where we share principles on dating God's way. It is one of the students' most favorite times because we get really raw, frank, and honest as we share some biblical principles for dating. We wanted to end this chapter by sharing those principles with you.

Hindsight is looking back at a situation that has already happened and evaluating if something went well or not. We used hindsight in analyzing our own relationship through the lens of the Bible to create these principles. They will help singles not only prepare themselves for marriage but do so without regret.

Principle 1: Value Yourself

There is a value deficit in both men and women today. We don't value others because we don't value ourselves. But here is the secret: You are worthy.

Men: The greatest temptation for a man is to be passive and lazy. We want to call all of you who are men to be mountain climbers and risk takers who are courageous. Deep down, you want to go to the greatest lengths to have that woman you desire to be your wife. Your goal is not to conquer women, but to conquer one woman by winning her heart in love. When you say yes to her, you must say no to all others.

Women: Are you worth being pursued? If the answer is yes (and it is), then wait and be pursued. The greatest temptation for a woman is to take control and take the lead. That's not attractive and not the way God intended it to be. God first pursued us, and our marriages are supposed to reflect Christ and the church (see Eph. 5:22).

Principle 2: Maximize Your Singleness

Do not seek a mate, but seek God. One of the meanings of the word *single* actually means to be consisting of a separate, unique whole.[4] So seek God to be made whole, and look for another person who is also whole, as you are. Again, you will attract what you are. Make a list of who you want to be and work toward that. Develop within you the character you are looking for, and eventually you will attract that type of person.

Instead of worrying about finding the right man or woman, work on being the right man or woman. This is the time to set in place a consistent life in God. It is your opportunity to be intentional about developing disciplined and consistent habits that will carry into your marriage to produce much fruit.

Principle 3: Do Not Pursue a Relationship until You're Ready for Marriage

Dating for sport is playing with people's hearts, which is both dangerous and sinful. The intent and purpose of dating is for marriage. If you desire to marry, you are in preparation right now. Every decision you make, both good and bad, will determine how prepared you are for when that time comes.

Treat the opposite sex as if they belong to someone else. Every person is first and foremost a child of God, so you should treat each other with honor and respect in speech, with eyes, and in friendship. Treat each other as you would like your future wife or husband to be treated, because they are in preparation for you.

Principle 4: He Initiates, She Responds

Finding a great life mate is an intentional pursuit. It is not like winning the lottery. Proverbs 31:10 says, *"A wife of noble character who can find?"* (NIV).

Men: Take initiative. Passivity in a man is not God's fault. Men should become proactive, intentional to find the woman they love. Hang around places you would want your future wife to be, and be intentional about pursuing her. The Bible tells young men to search for a woman of character. As we have said before, we are reminded that while looks won't last, godly character develops over time. It says nothing about feelings. This verse makes a woman's character the central characteristic of her suitability to be an excellent wife. Look for the diamonds!

Women: You are always teaching people how to treat you. Men won't value or respect you if you don't have respect for yourself and require something better from them. It is also helpful for you to hang out and spend time in places where a godly man would be. If you want a praying man, a prayer house is probably a good place to find a godly man, or a group where people are seeking after the Lord. Don't expect to find a man of character in a club or a bar.

Men: Pursue purity of heart and life. Become proactive, intentional, and find a woman of godly character.

Women: Pursue purity of heart and life. If you are interested in a man who is pursuing you, let him know where he stands with you.

Here are some helpful questions both men and women should be asking when considering a life mate:

Questions men need to ask:

1. Does she have noble character (see Prov. 31)?

2. Is she modest (see 1 Tim. 2:9)?

3. Will she follow your leadership?

4. Can you provide the lifestyle she expects?

5. Is she like the worst women in Proverbs (a nag, loud, quarreling, foolish, and unfaithful)?

6.   Is she a one-man woman?

7.   Do you want your daughters to be like her and your sons to marry someone like her?

Questions for women to ask:

1.   Do you want to help him and join his course of life (see Gen. 2:18; 1 Cor. 11:9)?

2.   Will he take responsibility for you and your children (see 1 Cor. 11:3)?

3.   Is he considerate and gentle with you (see 1 Pet. 3:7)?

4.   Will he be a good father (see Ps. 127:3-5; Eph. 6:4)?

5.   Is he a one-woman man (see 1 Tim. 3:2)?

6.   How valuable are you to him?

7.   Do you want your sons to be like him and daughters to marry someone like him?

Principle 5: Resurgence of Honor and Godly Counsel

In our culture, 18-year-olds are considered independent. However, the Bible says a man leaves his father and mother only to be joined to his spouse. Parents are responsible before God for their children, and so parents provide their children with a covering until they go under another one.

God promises that when we honor our parents "it will go well with us" (see Eph. 6:3). Your parents probably know you better than anyone else. If parental counsel is not an option for you, as we have said before, find a godly couple and ask them to mentor you.

When we honor others, especially those in authority over us, God is turned toward us.

While current dating standards have defined courtship as old-fashioned, it is the way of righteousness. Courting, when done right, can lay a foundation for a future of a successful marriage because the ways of God were followed during the premarital relationship.

Courtship was once known as a time for a young guy and girl to get know each other and each other's families. The young man would go to the parents of the woman of interest and ask permission to court their daughter, recognizing their authority and reaping the benefits of honor. The parents would then consider the proposal. This honored the position of the parent as the ones who are accountable for their child until they "leave and cleave to their spouse" (see Eph. 5:31). There was a time when it would have never been considered to do it any other way.

This form of courting produced honor, integrity, maturity, and accountability for both the guy and the girl. It brought value to each person involved. This is the most biblical model. The man is to be the pursuer, and by him going to the family and asking permission to court, he is taking the first step in demonstrating his ability to be a man who can lead.

Principle 6: Dating Redefined—Courtship

Like we have stated before, today's dating culture encourages people to practice separation and divorce. You start to not like someone anymore, so you separate, while it is likely you have already given your heart away to that person. God has made the fulfillment of intimacy to be a byproduct of commitment-based love. The joy of intimacy is the reward of commitment, not an emotional high. Once you decide on someone and marry them, you are in covenant with them for life. Love and romance in marriage, if done God's way, is like a good wine: it gets better with age.

Do not give your heart, passion, or physical intimacy away under any circumstances; guard it for your spouse. The Song of Songs says, "Do not arouse or awaken love until the time is right" (see 8:4). A guy and a girl should become romantically involved *only* if they plan to be married. A young man and a young woman should spend time with each other's families with the intention of marriage. This is true courtship.

The age-old process of courtship created protection and accountability with all involved. It does *not* have to end in marriage, but it should be entered into seriously with someone who is marriage potential. It is also a time to get to know each other safely in order to determine if marriage should be the outcome of the relationship. A courtship is successful whether or not marriage is the final result, because all was done with honor and protection, within the boundaries of a covering.

Principle 7: Have Reasonable Expectations

Even as you are not perfect, neither will you find someone who is perfect. We like to encourage young people to make a list of hopes and expectations to know what they are looking for in a future mate. It is important to turn that list on yourself, however, making sure you are the type of person you are looking for. Each of the items on that list are for you to aim for.

Proverbs 31:10 assumes that we are to be in a serious pursuit, actively engaging our minds to make a wise choice. We have seen both men and women have unbelievable expectations in physical features, financial stability, or other attributes. We are not saying to reach low, but sometimes our fairy-tale expectations are not worthy to be pursued. Sometimes they are simply vain imaginations.

We are to seek those who fear the Lord, honor Him, and honor our parents throughout the process. All of the other issues can be worked out if we have the drive, healthy communication, and great godly counsel.

Principle 8: Invest in a Relationship with Someone You Are Attracted to Entirely

Finally, invest your time in a person you find attractive physically, mentally, spiritually, emotionally, and in ministry gifts. We as a couple never wondered or ever had concerns about our values for children, biblical theology, or our mission in life. We were both in agreement in those things. Instead of focusing on the surface characteristics emphasized by our culture, we highly encourage young adults to find out about the all of the biblical characteristics of attraction when looking for a spouse.

These principles will help you walk out singleness in a way that honors God, yourself, and your future spouse. He will give grace as you war against the culture's way of dating and strive to grab a hold of His original design. If this is not the way you have done dating in the past, you can begin now!

Chapter 9

A PROPHETIC HOME

I will pour out of My Spirit on all flesh; your
sons and your daughters shall prophesy....
—Acts 2:17

Driving down I-40, from Phoenix to the Grand Canyon, Christelle and I spontaneously began to pray and speak in tongues. And out of that overflow, we began to pray for each other as husband and wife. This wasn't just praying for blessing and strength, as there was no great pressing need, but it was simply prophetic ministry over each other. The Holy Spirit began to give us pictures, images, impressions, and Scriptures for the other person. We had a great time, as this carried on for quite a while. We actually felt like we were getting to know each other on a deeper level as this was taking place.

When the prophetic spirit is in operation, it means that the testimony of Jesus is being spoken (see Rev. 19:10). This means that we understand, in a small measure, what Jesus thinks about another person, ministry, business, or location. In other words, prophecy is what God thinks about a situation, a circumstance, or a particular person.

The words spoken may not seem to reflect the natural circumstances at the time, but they are God's thoughts and they are what He is saying at that time (see Ps. 139). The opposite is also true. Satan's thoughts and words spoken over a person or a family are dark, while God's thoughts are full of light. Revelation 12:10 speaks of Satan, our enemy, being the *accuser of the brethren*. He hurls accusations about us before God's throne day after day and night after night. What would you rather come into agreement with—the prophetic spirit, which is the testimony of Jesus, or the accuser of humankind? We must choose to speak the testimony of Jesus over our marriages and families!

Today, prophesying over each other is now a normal part of our home, but it has not always been that way. At one time our home was a home focused on entertainment and the very thought of participating with the Holy Spirit and speaking prophetically was a foreign concept—it would have been preposterous.

Having a prophetic home may seem to be a strange concept to you. We are aware that the activity of the Holy Spirit, the third person of the Trinity, is often discussed, even hotly disputed. Does the Holy Spirit move today? How does He move if He does move today? These are all valid questions. Some believers in Christ assert that the gifts of the Holy Spirit ceased in the first century, which has caused much confusion and distortion. Many Christians have come to be convinced of this misconception simply through fear of the unknown, having never seen these gifts in operation. Some Christians are opposed to the idea because they have seen others manifest the power of the Holy Spirit in a way that seems embarrassing or strange. All of this has been instrumental in putting spiritual gifts on the fringes or relegating them as a thing of the past.

Out of fear, most people will move away from something that is unknown. Our personal conviction is that the subject of the activity of the Holy Spirit is unknown or misrepresented; therefore, fear has crept in and people stay away from knowing, agreeing with, and partnering with the Holy Spirit. But in doing so, many miss the benefits, tools, and gifts that the Holy Spirit desires to give to His people.

The Bible says that the manifestations of the Spirit are for the good of all and are given for everyone to operate in. We believe that understanding the prophetic and the coming great outpouring are crucial to building strong families. To us, it is so important for families to operate in the prophetic that we have devoted this whole chapter to this very topic.

END-TIME OUTPOURING

Before Jesus returns, there will be a great outpouring of the Holy Spirit. In this great revival, the Holy Spirit will release more miracles than those that were seen in the book of Acts and the book of Exodus combined, and they will be multiplied on a global scale. This will be the church's most glorious hour. Joel prophesied of the greatest outpouring of the Spirit in the end times (see Joel 2:28-32), where all the saints would receive dreams, visions, and angelic visitations. This outpouring will be manifested in many ways, but especially in the gift of prophecy. Peter quoted from Joel as he preached on the day of Pentecost:

> It shall come to pass in the last days, says God, that I
> will pour out of My Spirit on all flesh; your sons and
> your daughters shall prophesy.... I will pour out My

Spirit in those days; and they shall prophesy. I will show wonders in heaven above and signs in the earth beneath…. The sun shall be turned into darkness, and the moon into blood, before the coming of the great and awesome day of the Lord (Acts 2:17–20).

It will help us to look at some of the events that took place on the day of Pentecost to further understand the outpouring of the Spirit that is coming in the last days. During the outpouring on Pentecost, the Spirit fell on all those in the upper room and signs and wonders followed them. Thousands gathered to see what was taking place. The great sounds of wind, speaking in tongues, and the phenomena of praises to God in their own language all garnered a large audience. Peter stood up and preached the Gospel message that pierced hearts, and many were saved as a result: *"Then those who gladly received his word were baptized; and that day about three thousand souls were added to them"* (Acts 2:41).

Let us ask you a question: To what were they added? Were they added to a denomination? Were they added to the local network? How did they gather and continue to grow and nurture new believers? Luckily, Luke gives us the answer to this:

So continuing daily with one accord in the temple, and breaking bread from house to house, they ate their food with gladness and simplicity of heart, praising God and having favor with all the people. And the Lord added to the church daily those who were being saved (Acts 2:46-47).

The method of how the new believers were discipled was a simple formula. They met from house to house, meaning they met around food, fellowship, and teaching as a family. This was the structure that was already in place. The family is the great discipler, protector, accountability group, equipper, and trainer.

It is our conviction that God is preparing for not only a ministry of small groups, but also for families who meet and cultivate the presence of God continually in the home. Homes will have a fresh, alive spirit, where the Word of God is new, like the dew of the morning. We are speaking of a fresh baptism of fire being poured upon homes, where homes are on fire with the presence and reality of the Holy Spirit. We are talking about homes that are homes of prayer, altars of worship unto the one true God and not worshiping other gods.

What we are talking about is not easy to produce—these types of homes don't just happen. It is a countercultural lifestyle and a work of grace in the hearts and lives of God's people. These types of homes are only lived out with the help and strength of the Holy Spirit. God the Father gives us what we need through the gifts of His Holy Spirit. First Corinthians 14:1 declares, *"Pursue love, and desire spiritual gifts, but especially that you may prophesy."*

CONTENDING FOR A NEW TESTAMENT CULTURE

Jude wrote, *"I found it necessary to write to you exhorting you to contend earnestly for the faith which was once for all delivered to the saints"* (Jude 3). Mike Bickle said concerning this verse:

> The apostle Jude exhorted the believers under his leadership to fight earnestly to walk in the faith or in the quality of life in the Spirit that was originally given to the saints by the first apostles. Here are three areas in which we believe Jude is exhorting the believers to fight for.

1. We contend for New Testament doctrine in our understanding.

2. We contend for New Testament lifestyles, including purity, prayer and fasting (Matt. 5-7).

3. We contend for New Testament power in our life. In other words, we are to contend for a breakthrough of the fullness of God's power.[1]

The New Testament doctrine is significant, especially for the times in which we live. Biblical doctrines about sin, repentance, grace, redemption, salvation, Heaven, and hell have been greatly distorted and blurred in our day. We must contend earnestly to hold on to sound biblical doctrine rather than settle for a worldly, humanistic definition of truth. We need a theology that compels us to run from our sin into true freedom.

Contending to live in the *New Testament lifestyle* includes living a life of holiness, prayer, fasting, giving, and forgiving. In our current self-serving, religious culture, it seems like these basic doctrines are outdated and far from being grace-filled. Some may even say they are legalistic. This lifestyle is only lived out by the power of the Holy Spirit, but our agreement and our fierce determination to live this lifestyle are vitally important. Living like this cannot be viewed as being a casual happenstance; it requires an intentional removal of some things and subsequent replacement with other things that enrich and empower a specific vision. It's a *fight* to live our lives by the power of the Holy Spirit.

Lastly, we must fight earnestly to walk in *New Testament power*. The disciples walked in supernatural power that is also a part of the New Testament mandate for every believer. We are to contend to walk in the fullness of God's power. Again, it's a work of grace in our hearts, but it's also a partnership of our *yes* that God empowers. Just read Mark 16 and you will see that this mandate is not for some believers, but for all who believe:

> *And these signs will follow those who believe: In My name they will cast out demons; they will speak with new tongues; they will take up serpents; and if they drink anything deadly, it will by no means hurt them; they will lay hands on the sick, and they will recover* (Mark 16:17-18).

THEY WILL PROPHESY

When the Holy Spirit is poured out in the last days, the Bible says, *"They shall prophesy"* (Acts 2:18). One of the signs of God pouring out His Spirit will be prophecy on the lips of His people. It will not be relegated to *some* people, to only a few elite Christians. Rather, He will pour out His Spirit on all people—all flesh—and they will all prophesy.

Peter goes on to describe the ages that will receive this outpouring, both young and old, male and female—there is no one left out. The prophetic spirit will never be more apparent and greater than at this time in human history. The degree that we see the gift of prophecy in action today is such a small measure compared to what is coming in the days ahead.

THE CASE FOR PROPHECY TODAY

The church, from its inception on the day of Pentecost, was to be prophetic in nature. It is clear that the spirit of prophecy is potentially available to all (see Acts 2:17-18). Paul said, *"For you can all prophesy one by one, that all may learn and all may be encouraged"*

(1 Cor. 14:31). Steve Thompson, in his wonderful book *You May All Prophesy*, wrote, "Paul stated that all may prophesy. Jesus said that His sheep hear His voice. Prophecy in its most basic form is hearing what God is saying about someone and relaying it to them."[2]

There are various levels of prophecy and the strength and accuracy of the prophetic gifting. There is a significant distinction between simple prophecy and the office of a prophet. Some people mistakenly assume that you can only prophesy if you are a prophet. Simple prophecy, however, is limited to edification, exhortation, and comfort, and it is a gifting that every believer can function in.

Another point of confusion arises when people are afraid of prophecy, assuming that someone will see all the negative details of your life. For them, prophecy becomes something almost scary. In actual fact, however, someone who is operating in the office of the prophet may make corrections and establish directions for a ministry or nation, but only a few function in that office. To be recognized as someone who operates in the office of a prophet, one must have a proven history of giving specifics about future dates and events that come to pass.

Some operate in the office of the prophet and some operate in smaller measures of the prophetic anointing. The point of what we are saying is not to give special honor to some "elite" class of believers, but rather to emphasize that everyone can prophesy in some way or form. God is inviting all of us—every person, marriage, and home—to prophesy. We will break this down a little further.

Paul urged the church not to be ignorant about spiritual gifts: *"Now concerning spiritual gifts, brethren, I do not want you to be ignorant"* (1 Cor. 12:1). After a thorough study of spiritual gifts, we see that we as believers are commanded to operate in them. They are not optional. Again, Paul says, *"Therefore, brethren, desire earnestly to prophesy, and do not forbid to speak with tongues"* (1 Cor. 14:39). These are commands to be obeyed, not mere suggestions.

There is a tendency in the church to think that because we believe in something and talk about it occasionally, we are actively pursuing it ourselves. Over the past 100-plus years there has been a great resurgence in understanding the gifts of the Spirit. Yet many of the churches that used to contend for the use of the gifts are no longer actively using them today.

The health of the church depends on each member identifying and actively using his or her gifts for the good of the body. It is our personal conviction that the church starts in the home, as a family. The family is a reflection of how God has set up His Kingdom. Yes, it is much broader than just the nucleus of the family—of a father, mother, children, and grandparents. God intended for the strength of the church to be an overflow of the health of the home. A home that is on fire will set the church on fire!

A common misconception regarding spiritual gifts is that you have to reach a certain level of spiritual maturity before you can operate in them. We say it often, but our kids do not have a junior Holy Spirit. The gifts of the Spirit are available to all of us, and God uses our experiences, knowledge, and understanding to edify His church, using any willing, set-apart vessel to do so.

Our home is a testimony of the Holy Spirit's activity, even if it's just to a small degree. All of our kids speak in tongues, prophesy, pray for the sick, and operate in the prophetic spirit regularly. This is not an arrogant statement, but it is a testimony to Jesus and what He wants to do in every home. This is one of the reasons Paul reminded Timothy:

*Let no one despise your youth, but be an example to
the believers in word, in conduct, in love, in spirit, in
faith, in purity. Till I come, give attention to reading,
to exhortation, to doctrine. Do not neglect the gift that
is in you, which was given to you by prophecy with
the laying on of the hands of the eldership* (1 Timothy
4:12-14).

WHAT IS PROPHECY?

To operate in the prophetic spirit is to bring edification, exhortation, and comfort to each other. Paul said, *"But he who prophesies
speaks edification and exhortation and comfort to men"* (1 Cor. 14:3).
We will expand on each of these areas in order to create greater
clarity. Understanding this prophetic gifting is very important. If
someone is tearing someone down and calling it prophecy, he or
she is not truly operating in this gift, and the results can be harmful. God has invited us to operate in this gift with certain guidelines
to help protect us as well as those receiving this ministry.

- **Edification:** a building up; an improvement in
  knowledge. Edification speaks of building people
  up spiritually by confirming their destiny or special
  ministry focus (a singer, a school teacher, a marketplace leader, and so forth).

- **Exhortation:** to urge or to encourage someone to
  continue to persevere. Exhortation speaks of calling
  people to persevere and not give up on their promises in God in hard times, and to not give in to sin.
  We exhort people to persevere in their calling and
  in righteousness, telling them it is worth the trouble
  that they are enduring.

- **Comfort**: to give courage to them. Comfort speaks of giving God's perspective during great disappointment or setbacks in their lives, telling people that God has a plan in their situation.

We get a lot of people asking if prophecy is just encouraging people. While it is that, it is much more than that. Again, Steve Thompson writes, "Prophesying is speaking in order to strengthen, encourage and comfort others. However, prophecy is not just speaking human encouragement; it is speaking divine encouragement."[3]

HOW GOD SPEAKS

Mike Bickle, in his teaching "Receiving Words of Knowledge," says:

The language of the Spirit is impressions or pictures, which requires faith and weakness with humility to not overstate. Prophetic information is given most often as faint impressions such as:

1. **Mental pictures**: recurring impressions, pictures in our minds that indicate how the Lord will touch others. Some see the face of a person which represents a ministry direction.

2. **Emotional stirrings**: feeling various emotions like joy, sadness, or a burden for a person or a ministry as an indicator that the Lord will touch others related to that emotion or burden.

3. **Sympathetic pains**: feeling an unusual pain in a part of our bodies may indicate where the Lord

will touch others. A healing in a meeting is often an indicator of more of the same kind that the Lord wants to impart.

4. **Physical sensations:** experiencing the Spirit's presence (energy, heat, wind, etc.) in a specific area of our bodies is an indicator that the Lord desires to touch others.

The gifts often begin as the still small voice of God or as a subtle impression of the Spirit. It can be so subtle that many do not value it. Thus, they ignore it. As they value God's still small voice, they will be attentive to it. God's message is not always in the wind, but in the still small voice.[4]

God does speak in dramatic ways. But we often are looking for the dramatic, when most of the time He is speaking with a still small voice. That's why many times we have to dial down all those emotions and thoughts that distract us from focusing on what God is saying and doing. We must value the day of small beginnings, as we learn to be attentive to His voice and His subtle impressions, so we can speak them out and give expression to them.

GIFT OF PROPHECY THROUGH IMPERFECT PEOPLE

For now we see in a mirror, dimly, but then face to face. Now I know in part, but then I shall know just as I also am known (1 Corinthians 13:12).

In *Cultivating the Gifts*, Hall, Beauchamp, and Hackett propose, "The degree of accuracy with prophecy will depend upon the type of revelation given, the discernment skill level of the one receiving it, and also the quality of maturity in the person. Prophetic words will usually be a mixture as God gives us revelation that passes through our human 'filter' (our mind and heart), of which words can vary between 10% God's words and 90% our words. While it is possible to speak 100% accurate words from God, yet most often prophecy is a mixture."[5]

That is why we are called to weigh prophetic words as we test everything, while still holding fast to what is good without despising prophecy (see 1 Cor. 14:29; 1 Thess. 5:20-21). Another huge misconception is that prophetic words are 100 percent from God, when in fact they are not. At some point, from receiving the revelation to the interpreting and then to the application of them, they can be mixed with human thought and emotion. That's not to say it is bad, it's just not *all* God. God uses weak human beings to partner with His heart in giving edification, exhortation, and comfort to those around us, especially our families.

To help us, we have changed the wording from "God says" or "thus saith the Lord" to simply saying "this is what I feel" or "this is what I sense." After all, we know in part and prophesy in part. Using this language allows room for people to make mistakes, and we give them grace as we are all developing in this gift.

WHAT TO PRACTICALLY DO

Here are some things you can do in your home to welcome the Holy Spirit. We must welcome, we must invite, and we must honor the Holy Spirit's presence, asking Him for His leadership when we gather. It is important to take time to enter into worship to prepare our hearts for what God wants to do in our midst. We personally love praying in tongues for 5–15 minutes, sometimes more and sometimes less. We make sure cell phones, computers, the TV, and any other kind of distraction is put away. Then we engage in the following:

1. We ask for the Lord to release the gift of prophecy to each other.

2. We pray for the desire to encourage, edify, and exhort family members.

3. We ask for His testimony, His thoughts, and His desires for them.

4. We pray for the Holy Spirit to give us impressions, Scriptures, pictures, or phrases.

5. We also ask for revelation, interpretation, and application of the impressions or words He gives to us.

6. We ask the Lord for accuracy of interpretation and of His heart.

Think of it like this: "Functioning in the prophetic is like putting up the sail in a boat on a lake during a calm day. When it seems there is no breeze, the sail catches even the most gentle breeze that just barely moves the boat. However, it does move! A similar dynamic occurs when we ask the Lord what He is doing. We may not see a great move of the 'boat,' but it will often slightly move."[6]

Like we have said before, this is a normal part of our lives in our home. We have learned to love to ask for God's thoughts over our lives, home, and children. Even when we are busy, we try to make time for this activity because we enjoy it so much. It is so powerful when we have times of worship and ministry like this.

I (Antonio) have seen the results of the power of prophecy when I speak prophetically into my family. When I speak some of God's thoughts, I not only get to know my children and wife better, but I am able to speak into them life, power, and grace. It seems the strength that comes from me as a father and husband is much deeper, and the impact is greater upon the hearts of my family because it was me who spoke. We also love it when our children prophetically minister to us, as it is such a powerful time. Our children get to know their parents during this time, and they get to partner with God.

Our children also get to prophesy over each other. Recently, our son Gabriel was prophesying over our other son Elijah. Gabriel prophetically saw that Elijah was praying at night, when no one else was looking. He said, "You even do it under your sheets." Gabriel declared, "God sees and likes it."

Elijah turned to Gabriel shocked and said, "How did you know?"

Gabriel responded, "I didn't know. I saw it." Another time, Gabriel again was praying over Isabella and said, "You're a servant. You help us a lot and we don't know it." This word changed our son's image of his sister for the better. He got to know his sister the way God sees her and it changed his and the other brothers' perspective of her.

FRESH BAPTISM OF FIRE IN YOUR HOME

I came to send fire on the earth, and how I wish it were already kindled! But I have a baptism to be baptized with, and how distressed I am till it is accomplished! (Luke 12:49-50)

Jesus's longing was to fill human beings with the fire of the Holy Spirit. The ultimate goal of redemption is to have a people fully filled with the life of God by the presence of the Holy Spirit.

God wants to make His home in us and in our homes. By the Holy Spirit, both the Father and Son make their home within us. He wants human beings to be the very temple of God, the dwelling place of the Almighty.

God fills us with the fire of His Spirit to burn out all opposition to love. It is the ministry of love whereby all other lovers who compete for our affections are vanquished for the incomparable pleasures of loving God and His glory. It is to be caught up into one vehement flame of love. Possessing God's fire is to brave the whirlwind of God and dare to approach the inapproachable light and fiery blaze of divine love, where nothing perverse or ugly makes it through the flame.

There is nothing you can do in your own strength, no matter what state your home is in or what state your marriage is in. The Bible clearly says in Zechariah 4:6: *"Not by might nor by power, but by My Spirit,' says the Lord of hosts."* There are some good things to be found in counseling, but we believe that every home needs the fire of the Holy Spirit. It may be that you are trying to do things too much in your own strength; or it may be you are trying to fix your marriage that may need a lot of work, and you may have made so many mistakes in your home that they seem unfixable. Outside of the fire and power of the Holy Spirit, it is impossible, but with Him all things are possible!

SIMPLY ASK HIM

Jesus said:

> *Which of you fathers, if your son asks for a fish, will give him a snake instead? Or if he asks for an egg, will give him a scorpion? If you then, though you are evil, know how to give good gifts to your children, how*

much more will your Father in heaven give the Holy
Spirit to those who ask Him! (Luke 11:11-13 NIV)

We love how this verse starts out speaking to fathers, *"Which*
of you fathers...." It is almost like He is having a family meeting,
speaking directly to fathers and homes. This is the start of asking
for the power and infilling of the Holy Spirit in our lives, marriages, and families. We must know that this is a family discussion
for believers—His sons and daughters.

In order to be filled with the baptism of the Holy Spirit, there
are two things we must do. First, we must ask Him for the infilling. This is not asking our heavenly Father for salvation; instead, it
pertains to an infilling of the Holy Spirit released to His children.
R.A. Torrey says, "The Baptism with the Holy Spirit is a work of
the Holy Spirit separate and distinct from His regenerating Work.
To be regenerated by the Holy Spirit is one thing, to be baptized
with the Holy Spirit is something different, something further."[7]

Second, we are to receive the Holy Spirit. We must ask
expecting to receive from our good Father. John Bevere writes,
"Throughout the book of Acts, the infilling of the Spirit is typically followed by an outward manifestation that could be seen and
heard—most commonly in the form of tongues and prophecy.
This is why the apostles would often say that the Holy Spirit would
'come upon' believers."[8]

We believe your home can be a home set on fire. Your home
can be a place of His presence, where it's not a one-time event or
a thing of the past, but something that should be pursued for a
deeper and increased level of His presence and power. We invite
you to allow the Holy Spirit to move in your life and home. We
invite you to move in agreement with the prophetic spirit in your
home today. After all, revival begins in the home!

Chapter 10

A THOUSAND GENERATIONS

Live a generational lifestyle. The direction you travel today
will pave the way for your children's journey tomorrow.
—Don Nori*

There are countless books on how to build a strong marriage and family. These books will strengthen communication, build trust, help with crises, and much more in our relationships. Although these are good and profitable, these resources are focused much of the time on you, your marriage, and your family. Rarely do they consider future generations. This brings us to the question: Is your marriage and family only about you? Did you ever consider that your marriage and family could affect the next generation? Perhaps our lives and homes would be different if we thought about an entire family line rather than just our own immediate family.

Most newly married couples rarely contemplate or forecast their future grandchildren and great-grandchildren's lives. Beyond a romantic fantasy of what their grandchildren may look like, a deliberate, strategic vision for building a lasting legacy is seldom in their minds. Once a person hits 50, however, these thoughts become more frequent as reality begins to set in.

Many of us are too shortsighted in our thinking when it comes to thinking generationally. God thinks eternally. He sees and thinks generationally, toward building a lasting heritage and leaving a legacy for others to follow. In our temporal mind we hardly put the effort into leaving a lasting spiritual legacy for generations to come. We think we enter into eternity when we die, but if we're breathing today, our eternity has already started. Time is infinite, constant, and unstoppable. It is a dimension in which our past and present are congruent with eternity. They are not separate entities. We're living in eternity right now, and how we live our life today will affect our eternity and the eternity for the next generations.

God said through Isaiah, *"My righteousness will be forever, and My salvation from generation to generation"* (Isa. 51:8). Salvation from God is generational. How long is a generation? Some say 20 years, while others say a generation is 30 years. Others speculate the length of a generation to be 70 or even 100 years. And there are some who are convinced it is 40 years, because that is how long the Israelites wandered in the wilderness.

Generations, in the sense of family, usually refer to the difference in age or the age gap between grandparents, parents, and children. When God made His covenant with Abraham or David, it was an everlasting covenant. He made it generationally and eternally, not just with one person. The fulfillment of God's covenant was and is made to be fulfilled generationally, even in spite of those generations that are faithless. Solomon, the son of David, reaped the blessings of being king. His acquisition of wealth, power, and even building the great temple further demonstrated the fulfillment of God's promise to David's family. Solomon literally stood on the shoulders of his father David, and if he would continue to walk in his father's footsteps, his family would continue to reign. God said:

> Now if you walk before Me as your father David walked, in integrity of heart and in uprightness, to do according to all that I have commanded you, and if you keep My statutes and My judgments, then I will establish the throne of your kingdom over Israel forever, as I promised David your father, saying, "You shall not fail to have a man on the throne of Israel" (1 Kings 9:4-5).

LEGACY

Webster's defines *legacy* as "a gift by will, especially of money or other personal property, something transmitted by or received from an ancestor or predecessor or from the past."[1] Some couples desire to leave a financial inheritance for their children. They save, invest, and ensure their children receive the benefits of their life's work. Most of the time, this is what we think of when we think about leaving an inheritance or a legacy. Some families are able to perpetuate their family's success for two or three generations, and sometimes even longer. Other families end up in a reoccurring financial abyss, criminal records, divorce, sickness, and much more. Why is that?

The reality is, as Ledbetter and Bruner state in *Family Legacy*, "No matter who we are, where we live, or what our goals may be, we all have one thing in common: a heritage. That is, a financial, emotional and spiritual legacy passed on from parent to child. Every one of us is passed a heritage, lives out a heritage, and gives a heritage to our family. It's not an option. Parents always pass to their children a legacy…good, bad or some of both."[2] What does the Bible say about leaving a legacy and an inheritance? We want to see how God views our marriage and families, and line up with His vision.

GENERATIONAL VIEW

Therefore know that the Lord your God, He is God, the faithful God who keeps covenant and mercy for a thousand generations with those who love Him and keep His commandments (Deuteronomy 7:9).

For I, the Lord your God, am a jealous God, visiting the iniquity of the fathers upon the children to the third and fourth generations of those who hate Me (Exodus 20:5).

God shows His character in these verses. He is faithful and true. The promise stands first as God's choice of showing mercy for a thousand generations to those who walk in affection-based obedience. God chooses to invite His people by kindness, compelling them to obedience motivated by love. The word *mercy* is coupled with *covenant* so that we may know the reward of knowing Him. God deals through the eyes of covenant agreement, and His commands are the terms. He is faithful to His covenant of mercy toward us and to a thousand generations after us. He is overwhelmingly generous. God is not a dictator but a wholehearted lover who desires affection-based obedience out of voluntary love.

In Exodus 20:5, God explains and gives some descriptions of His justified action for those who hate Him and who stand against Him. He first states that He will *visit the iniquity of the fathers*. The word *visit* is important to look at here—he does not desire to stay, leaving a lasting curse, but will indisputably visit in hopes for turning a heart.

Similarly, when Pharaoh would not let the Israelites go, God sent Moses to pronounce to everyone in Egypt that God would go through Egypt at midnight and all the firstborn sons would die (see Exod. 11:4-8). This was the first Passover. The angel of the Lord killed all firstborn males, human and animal alike, of every household, except for those in the homes that were marked as God had instructed them.

The head of each Israelite household was responsible for the arrangements for his family. At sundown, a young lamb was to be slain by the head of the household, or a child was to be slain by the angel of death. This principle still holds true today. Blessings and curses are passed down from the father.

INIQUITY PASSED DOWN

Let's continue to look at this verse further: *"Visiting the iniquity of the fathers upon the children to the third and fourth generations of those who hate Me"* (Exod. 20:5). We should pause for a second to define some words that can get confusing if we don't properly understand them. Sometimes, it seems that sin, transgression, and iniquity are used interchangeably. Let us define more clearly what they are. Marilyn Hickey writes, "Sin means to miss the mark. A transgression means to trespass or overstep pre-established boundaries. Lastly, the word iniquity means 'to bend' or 'to distort' (the heart)."[3] To have iniquity passed down from the father means to have a bent toward something. It's a predisposition of sin that gets passed down from one person to the next. If a sin is repeated without repentance, it will inherently be passed down to the next generation through the bloodline. When a person continually transgresses past a pre-established boundary, iniquity is handed down to the offspring. The offspring will have the same kind of weakness, and many times the weakness will increase in the next generation.

Marilyn Hickey and Sarah Bowling write in another book: "Here, in a few brief lines, is a picture of God's balanced justice. On the one hand, we have God's mercy, patience, and an abundance of goodness, truth, mercy, and forgiveness. On the other hand, God allows the iniquity of a person to be visited upon that person's heir. The sins of the fathers are passed down because they have not been cleared. This is a vitally important concept for you to understand. The way we are set free from the iniquity of the fathers is God's merciful and generous forgiveness."[4]

FATHER'S BLESSINGS VERSUS THE FAMILY CURSE

Throughout this book we have referenced Jonathan Edwards several times, as there is much to learn from his life. We want to reiterate his family line here and compare it with another American family to illustrate the power of generational curses and blessings.

Max Jukes was an atheist who married a godless woman. Some 560 descendants were traced.

Three hundred of Max Jukes descendants cost the United States government more than $1.25 million in the 19th century. His lineage cost more than $1,000 a person, including all men, women, and children, from poverty and crime.

Here are a few more facts about this family. Three hundred and ten of the 1,200 descendants were professional poor people, or more than one in four. They lived in poorhouses equivalent to 2,300 years.

Three hundred of the 1,200, or one in four, died in infancy from lack of good care and good conditions. There were 50 women who lived lives of notorious debauchery. Four hundred men and women were physically wrecked early by their own wickedness. There were seven murderers. Sixty were habitual thieves who each spent on average 12 years in lawless havoc. There were 130 criminals who were convicted of crime.[5]

FAMILY BLESSINGS

In comparison, as revealed in chapter 3, the life of Jonathan Edwards did not resemble his contemporary Max Jukes in the least bit. Edwards was a committed Christian, who married a godly young lady, and together they left a tremendous legacy—college graduates, college presidents and professors, U.S. senators, state governors, ministers to foreign countries, a controller of the U.S. Treasury, judges, lawyers, a dean of a law school, officers in the military, missionaries, preachers, authors, and even a vice president of the United States.[6]

Jonathan Edwards died at age of 56, and his wife died just a few weeks later. Jonathan and Sarah Edwards probably did not leave a large financial legacy; they did, however, impart to their children an intellectual capacity and vigor, moral character, and devotion to God that projected them through generations without losing the strength and force of their great ancestry.

THE LAW OF BLESSING AND CURSES

Most individuals and families are living out previous *blessings* and *curses*, whether they know it or not. In reference to this, Derek Prince writes, "Both of them are vehicles of supernatural power. It's very important to understand we're not dealing with something that's purely natural. It goes beyond the natural. They are vehicles of supernatural power for good if they're blessings, for evil if they're curses. And one characteristic feature of them is that very frequently they'll continue on from generation to generation."[7]

> *Now it shall come to pass, if you diligently obey the voice of the Lord your God, to observe carefully all His commandments which I command you today, that the Lord your God will set you high above all nations of the earth. And all these blessings shall come upon you and overtake you, because you obey the voice of the Lord your God* (Deuteronomy 28:1-2).

In this portion of Deuteronomy 28, the blessings and curses are cataloged at length and in various details. This deals exclusively with blessings and curses—14 verses of blessings and 54 verses of curses.

Before the Israelites entered into the land of promise, their whole destiny was laid before them, and it all depended upon their obedience or disobedience. Many might look at these verses and try to dismiss them because they come from the Old Testament. However, these verses still hold true today. Pronouncements of favor and blessing were to follow them if they *fully* obeyed God's voice and ways. Blessings would come upon their finances, children, physical bodies, and everything they touched. God reaffirms His intention to make Israel an exalted and holy people.

However, these promises are conditional and link blessing with obedience. God is showing His extraordinary desire to abundantly bless them and for that blessing to continue to a thousand generations. The blessings of God are hinged upon loving Him through affection-based obedience. Obeying God is definitely connected with loving Him. Some may read that and counterargue by saying we are not interpreting God's love correctly or we are not filled with grace.

The Western "God makes me happy" mindset, regardless of how we live, is incorrect and unbiblical. God spits us out if we are lukewarm; He cuts down trees that don't bear fruit. He deals harshly with those who show hatred and disdain for His ways all through Scripture. God is the same yesterday, today, and forever, regardless of how we want Him to be. Deuteronomy continues:

> *But it shall come to pass, if you do not obey the voice of the Lord your God, to observe carefully all His commandments and His statutes which I command you today, that all these curses will come upon you and overtake you* (Deuteronomy 28:15).

Moses goes on to list the curses on the people if God's commands are not observed. The list of curses includes the loss of prosperity, disease, barrenness, contagious epidemics, defeat, and exile—a reversal of roles between Israel and the nations. Rather than Israel leading, they would become servants and slaves. In effect, covenant violation would undo the Exodus and deliver the nation back into the pains of bondage.

Physical curses being passed down are very real; they are not just a spiritual principle but a physical law that even the world understands. Have you been to a doctor's office or filled out an insurance form of any kind? They usually ask for your parents' and grandparents' physical history—what types of diseases they have or had and their causes of death—because they understand that their problems are in your background and you could have them too. The sins of the fathers really do get passed down.

Regarding this, Marilyn Hickey writes, "The phenomena of a generational curse is like this: One person practices a certain sin (alcoholism, violence, sexual sin, etc.), until it becomes a lifestyle. Once entrenched the sin becomes an iniquity—a weakness toward a certain behavior. That behavior is practiced over and over allowing Satan to gain control of the mind, will, and emotions. That control will continue for that individual and consequently future generations becoming a generational curse."[8]

These curses from iniquities being passed down have to be dealt with. The only way to deal with them is through repentance and allowing the blood of Jesus to cover our lives and homes. Derek Prince says regarding this, "Through the sacrifice of Jesus on the cross we have passed out from under the curse and entered into the blessing of Abraham whom God blessed in all things."[9]

John writes, *"If we walk in the light, as he is in the light, we have fellowship with one another, and the blood of Jesus, his Son, purifies us from all sin"* (1 John 1:7 NIV). Jesus became the sacrifice for us: *"He was wounded for our transgressions, He was bruised for our iniquities"* (Isa. 53:5). He paid the price for sin, iniquity, and transgressions, and by His blood our family line can be clean.

We are commanded to repent. Jesus said, *"I tell you, no; but unless you repent you will all likewise perish"* (Luke 13:3). Repentance is changing the direction of your home and life vision, which is vital if we are going to execute Isaiah 53 in our homes. We need the blood of Jesus to mark the doorposts of our home so that we stop the curses from continuing in our family lines. Without repentance, the blood of Jesus does not take effect.

Jeremiah says, *"The fathers have eaten sour grapes, and the children's teeth are set on edge"* (Jer. 31:29; see also Ezek. 18:2). What are sour grapes? Don Nori says they are the character qualities or the inclinations "toward certain behaviors that are handed down in families through the generations. Some might call them generational sins or familiar spirits. Whatever they are, our children should not have to deal with them! We are in Christ, and as children of God, we want His heritage and His character traits to rule us, not our own sin nature or the sins of our fathers."[10]

BUILD FOR THE NEXT GENERATION

In Genesis 7, God instructs Noah to build a boat. How crazy was that? God was angry at the sin that was being committed and that was growing increasingly wicked day after day. The longer humankind was alive, the more they sought after greater levels of sin. Humankind had become like animals rather than God's image-bearing children. They did what was right in their own eyes, and, having no fear of God, destruction and misery had become their way. God's response to all of the wickedness was this verdict: *"My Spirit shall not strive with man forever"* (Gen. 6:3).

God simply grew impatient and tired of humanity's sin. The degrading and disgusting sin of man resulted in judgment. God would not shield His beloved people anymore. Because that immoral race had filled up the measure of their iniquities, He was about to introduce a display of His justice (see Eccl. 8:11). The God of mercy looked for a way out for man. His enduring love was still there. He found Noah, a righteous man, and these were His directions to him:

Make yourself an ark of gopherwood (Genesis 6:14).

Then the Lord said to Noah, "Come into the ark, you and all your household, because I have seen that you are righteous before Me in this generation" (Genesis 7:1).

This is a prophetic picture of the generation that we live in today. By faith Noah built a home for himself and his family. Noah's entire family was saved, even his son Ham, who was not a man of character. This shows us how God views the family structure. In Genesis 6:18, God still desired to keep His covenant with Noah: *"I will establish My covenant with you; and you shall go into the ark—you, your sons, your wife, and your sons' wives with you."*

Are you building for the generations after you? The generation we live in today is becoming more and more ungodly with its intolerance to Jesus and His ways. Are you teaching your children what kind of people they ought to be? What type of spouses they ought to marry? Are you training your children in God's truth? Are you creating a biblical identity in your children and grandchildren so they don't waiver with the spirit of this age, full of lust, perversion, humanistic worship of self, and other attacking bombardments? Is your home a home of prayer, His presence, and His Word? If it is not, we urge you: this is how you build for the next generation. This is how you establish God's Kingdom for a lasting heritage. God is looking for the righteous leaders who will keep His covenant.

We must not be content to have Christianity for ourselves. We must not be content that our prayer times are only focused on meeting our personal needs. Are you interceding for your entire family lineage? Do you view yourself as the patriarch of the generations to come? God is acknowledged as being the God of Abraham, Isaac, and Jacob (see Exod. 3:6). Do you see yourself as Abraham? May God say your name there, as the God of your family!

God is into blessing generations, not just individuals. When God blesses, He abundantly blesses way beyond the man. He's an extravagant giver of blessings to those who love Him, *"showing love to a thousand generations of those who love me and keep my commandments"* (Exod. 20:6 NIV).

GOD'S COVENANT

God made an everlasting covenant with Abraham and his descendants. Abraham would prove to be the father of those who believe. This is the promise of what God calls an everlasting covenant. What is remarkable is the assurance that God is faithful to Abraham's seed as much as He was faithful to him. This promise is the same for the children as for the parent. He will make an everlasting covenant with the next generation.

> *And I will establish My covenant between Me and you and your descendants after you in their generations, for an everlasting covenant, to be God to you and your descendants after you. Also I give to you and your descendants after you the land in which you are a stranger, all the land of Canaan, as an everlasting possession; and I will be their God* (Genesis 17:7-8).

The certainty of God's promises rest on God's free mercy and generosity. He is faithful to His purpose, and His faithfulness is the foundation on which the promise rests. His promise is eternal, not temporal. The conditions of His covenant in each case are the same: it is offered to the faith of the parent, and it has to be accepted by faith alone. It must be believed. But at the same time, in one act of believing and obedience, the man and wife are taking hold of God's richest blessings, not only for them but also for their family and the generations after them.

What a great covering we can leave for our children. Our heart's desire for our own family is that our children would not be "barely" believing Christians, but that they would stand on the shoulders which we fought so hard to have. And then our grandchildren can stand tall on their shoulders, and on and on it goes. This can only be done if we, the parents or grandparents reading this, contend for that, believing in faith for our home, family, and the future generations. This is a mighty battle that takes contending in prayer, a life of faithfulness, and a fear of God brought into our homes.

Consecrate Your Family

He decreed statutes for Jacob and established the law in Israel, which he commanded our ancestors to teach their children, so the next generation would know them, even the children yet to be born, and they in turn would tell their children. Then they would put their trust in God and would not forget his deeds but would keep his commands. They would not be like their ancestors—a stubborn and rebellious generation, whose hearts were not loyal to God, whose spirits were not faithful to him (Psalm 78:5-8 NIV).

This history of what God has done has to be handed down to the next generation. God instructed the Israelites to teach God's ways and Israel's history to their children so that the new generation would not go astray as their ancestors did. We must share the sins we committed in the past and how God set us free from the bondage of sin. We must tell them of our previous stubborn and rebellious ways that we once had, and tell them of God's goodness. We must teach them the principles of His Word, that they might be known and observed by our children. The older generation is unquestionably required to teach their children about God's mighty deeds in their family's history.

We have personally gone through some difficult seasons, and because we had a prophetic history with God, we knew what to do. The Word of God has everything that we need for every season and challenge of life. The forefathers are to teach the next generation of His goodness, His power, and His majesty.

CONGRUENCE OF GENERATIONS

There is usually a sequence of Christianity in a family lineage, which is clearly seen throughout history. Usually the first generation Christian commits and gives his or her life to Christ, humbly surrendering their life to Jesus and living by God's truth. They have children and *assume* their kids will also walk in God's ways, until they get older and their faith is tested. Some stay in God's ways, but many do not. Sometimes, the following generation walks completely away from God—they lose the faith of their forefathers altogether. This should not be a surprise—without the forefathers passing their faith and firmly establishing it, there will be no inward conversion and therefore no conviction to live differently. This is a tragedy. We cannot *assume* that the next generation will follow God and walk in His ways. We must teach them.

Individuals, marriages, families, and even nations go through cycles of belief, conviction, assumption, and a turning away of some kind. This is best explained by Alexander Tyler, a Scottish history professor at the University of Edinburgh in 1787, who researched the fall of the Athenian Republic some 2,000 years earlier. He stated:

> The average age of the world's greatest civilizations from the beginning of history has been about 200 years. During those 200 years, these nations always progressed through the following sequence:

1.   From bondage to spiritual faith;

2.   From spiritual faith to great courage;

3.   From courage to liberty;

4.   From liberty to abundance;

5.   From abundance to complacency;

6.   From complacency to apathy;

7.   From apathy to dependence;

8.   From dependence back into bondage.[11]

In reference to Tyler's research, where is your family in this cycle? Take serious measure of this. Have you told the next generation what God has done in your life and marriage? Have you told them of the truths found in the Scriptures? Do they know them? We have a serious mandate and obligation to teach the generations God's redemptive history and ways to live for the future so that their faith is firmly established. We can't assume the next generation will get it; they won't automatically.

This 200-year cycle is not only for nations, but also for marriages and families. Through the years we easily can forget what God has done. That is why the Sabbath rest and the various festivals are so critical to celebrate as a family. Remind yourself of what God has done through sharing testimonies and teaching the Word.

The psalmist declared, *"One generation shall praise Your works to another"* (Ps. 145:4). It is up to the parents to share the goodness of God's wonders to the next generation. This is not a duty, but a privilege. The acts that God has done throughout your life should be told. Make sure your children know of His goodness. They will hold on to your testimony as their own, because, after all, they come from you.

WHAT IS THE VISION FOR YOUR FAMILY?

We want to end this book by asking you one of the most important questions that should lead you to prayer and long discussions. Here is the question: What is the vision for your family? Proverbs 29:18 says, *"Where there is no vision, the people are unrestrained"* (NASB). When you don't have a vision, you will not plan for anything. In fact, you will be the victim of crisis and circumstance. Being casualties of the winds of events is not how we are to live our lives. That person, marriage, and family will live undisciplined and unbridled. Without a vision, people break out of control—they live wild. In order to counter this truth, we need a vision, clearly written, stated, and lived out. You need a target to hit, a mark to point your arrows to.

We want to encourage each marriage and family to have a prophetic vision. This vision will guide you. It will call you back to God and His ways if you happen to divert. This vision should be done with the end in mind, considering the generations.

A strong nation clearly writes down its constitution, its values, and what it stands for. These will help guide a nation when things come into question, when things get difficult, or if they get distracted. If a nation does this, so should an individual, a married couple, and a family. Christelle and I don't believe it's optional. Without it you will easily get distracted and deterred from what you should be focusing on. From this vision, your mission will probably have to be revisited and refreshed over time. Take time to consider this vision. Take time to dream. Take time to pray over this. Invite your children to participate, if they are old enough.

Let us end this book, then, leaving you with this testimony. Much of what we are experiencing and living out today came from first writing down our own hopes and dreams. In 2008, we were on a long drive, and we wrote down desires for our marriage, family, and ministry, many of which we have already lived out. Our sights were set too low, however. We have gone back and rewritten what we feel God has called our marriage to contend for and dream about, our family to aim at, and our ministry to extend to. Thank God that He sees much more than we do.

He has placed desires and hopes within each one of us to live out. They may seem impossible today, but like us, you too will experience this prophetic vision. Write it down and contend to live it out. We pray that God would bless and strengthen your union and the fruit of your marriage for a thousand generations!

ENDNOTES

INTRODUCTION

* This quote is accessed from The Spurgeon Archive, http://www.spurgeon.org/revival.htm.

1. Harry S. Truman, "Public Papers of the Presidents: Independence Day Address," Harry S. Truman Library & Museum, http://www.trumanlibrary.org/publicpapers/index.php?pid=1949.

CHAPTER 1
COUNTERCULTURAL

* Rod Parsley: *Silent No More* (Lake Mary, Florida: Charisma House, A Strang Company, Kindle Edition, 2005), 101.

1. Richard Toye, *The Roar of the Lion* (Great Claredon Street, Oxford: Oxford Press, 2013), 41.

2. Definition of the word *culture*, accessed from Dictionary.com, http://dictionary.reference.com/browse/culture.

3. Andrew Fletcher, "John Bartlett Familiar Quoations," Bartleby.com, http://www.bartleby.com/100/199.html.

4. Alvin J. Schmidt, *Under the Influence* (Grand Rapids, Michigan: Zondervan, 2001), 48.

5. Voddie T. Baucham Jr., *Family Driven Faith* (Wheaton, Illinois: Crossway, 2007), 23.

6. Ibid., 23.

7. This was accessed from Knot Yet, www .twentysomethingmarriage.org.

8. Carol Morello, "Study: Delaying marriage hurts middle-class Americans most," *The Washington Post*, March 15, 2013, www.washingtonpost.com.

9. Brian Dickerson, "Look who's redefining marriage now (not same-sex couples)," *Detroit Free Press*, March 31, 2013, http:// www.freep.com.

10. Karen Swallow Prior, "The Case for Getting Married Young," *The Atlantic*, March 22, 2013, www.theatlantic.com.

11. Prior, "The Case for Getting Married Young."

12. Patricia H. Shiono, Linda Sandham Quinn, *Journal Issue: Children and Divorce*, 1994. www.futureofchildren.org.

13. Albert Mohler quoted in Voddie T. Baucham Jr., *Family Driven Faith*, 24.

14. Ibid.

15. Charles Krauthammer, *Things That Matter* (New York: Crown Publishing, 2013), 154.

16. Germaine Greer, *The Female Eunuch* (Australia: HarperCollins, 1970, e-book), 4991.

17. Gary Thomas, *Sacred Marriage* (Grand Rapids, Michigan: Zondervan, 2000), 22.

18. Ibid., 23.

CHAPTER 2
ESTABLISHING FOUNDATIONS

* Billy Graham, *Day by Day* (Minneapolis, MN: World Wide, 1965), May 14.

1.   Derek Prince, *Husbands and Fathers* (Grand Rapids, MI: Chosen Books, a division of Baker Publishing Group, 2000), 23.

2.   Gary Chapman, *The Marriage You Always Wanted* (Chicago, Illinois: Moody Publishers, 2005, 2009), 17.

3.   Prince, *Husbands and Fathers*, 23.

4.   Chapman, *The Marriage You Always Wanted*, 11.

5.   Gary Thomas, *Sacred Marriage* (Grand Rapids, Michigan: Zondervan, 2000), 31.

6.   Andreas J. Kosternberger with David W. Jones, *God, Marriage, and Family: Rebuilding the Biblical Foundation* (Wheaton, Illinois: Crossway, 2004), 71.

7.   Ibid., 76.

8.   Ibid., 78.

9.   Derek Prince, *Marriage Covenant* (New Kensington, PA: Whitaker House, 1978, 2006), 540.

10. Ibid., 587.

11. Definition of the word *intimus*, Mera English.com, http://www.meraenglish.com/2013/10/16/origin-of-intimate/ .

12. Gary Chapman, *The Family You've Always Wanted* (Chicago, Illinois: Northfield Publishing, 2008), Loc 363.

13. Derek Prince, *God Is a Matchmaker* (Bloomington, Minnesota: Chosen Books, 1986, 2011), 14.

14. Prince, *Husbands and Fathers*, 25.

15. Ibid., 68

16. John Bevere, *Honor's Reward* (New York, NY: Faith Words, 2007), 106–107.

17. Richard D. Phillips, *The Masculine Mandate: God's Calling to Men* (Lake Mary, FL: Reformation Trust Publishing, 2010), 171.

18. Ibid., 186.

19. Ibid., 142.

20. Dr. Emerson Eggerichs, *Love and Respect* (Nashville, Tennessee: Thomas Nelson, 2004), 14–15.

21. Tony Evans, *For Married Men Only: Three Principles for Loving Your Wife* (Chicago: Moody Publishers. 2010), 7.

22. Tony Evans, *For Married Women Only: Three Principles for Honoring Your Husband* (Chicago: Moody Publishers 2010, Kindle Edition), 47.

23. Elisabeth Elliot, *Let Me Be A Woman* (Wheaton, Illinois: Tyndale House Publishers, Inc. 1976), 90.

24. Ibid., 88.

25. Evans, *For Married Women Only*, 43.

26. Prince, *Husbands and Fathers*, 48–49.

27. Ibid., 50.

CHAPTER 3
THE FIGHT FOR MARRIAGE

* John and Stasi Eldredge, *Love and War* (New York: Doubleday Religion, 2009), 31.

1. Elliot, *Let Me Be A Woman*, 97.

2. Eldredge, *Love and War*, 98.

3. Bob and Audrey Meisner, *Marriage Undercover: Thriving in a Culture of Quiet Desperation* (Raleigh, NC: MilesStones

International Publishers, Kindle Edition, March 16, 2011), 1016–1020.

4.   Ibid., 169–170.

5.   Kostenberger, *God, Marriage, and Family*, 25.

6.   Focus on the Family, The *Best Advice I ever Got on Marriage* (Brentwood, Tennessee: Worthy Publishing, 2012), 47.

7.   Ibid., 48.

8.   Doreen Moore, "Jonathan Edwards: Ministry and the Life of the Family," The Resurgence, http://theresurgence.com/files/pdf/doreen_moore _1995-07_jonathan_edwards--ministry _and_the_life_of_the _family.pdf, 1.

9.   Lyle Dorsett, *A Passion for God: The Spiritual Journey of A. W. Tozer* (Chicago, Illinois: Moody Publishers, 2008, Electronic Edition), 2385–2412.

10. Roberts Liardon, *God's Generals: Why They Succeeded and Why Some Failed* (New Kensington, PA: Whitaker House, 1996), 180.

11. Ibid., 181.

12. Ibid., 182.

13. Ibid., 189–190.

14. Ibid., 190.

15. John Maxwell, *Today Matters* (New York, NY: Warner Faith, 2004), 107.

16. Diane Severance, "Jonathan Edwards: America's Humble Giant," Christianity.com, http://www.christianity.com/church/church-history/timeline/1701-1800/jonathan-edwards -americas-humble-giant-11630188.html, 2.

17. Moore, "Jonathan Edwards: Ministry and the Life of the Family," 2.

18. George Mardsen, *A Life of Jonathan Edwards* (New Haven and London: Yale University Press, 2003), 6770.

19. Ibid., 6785.

20. Severance, "Jonathan Edwards: America's Humble Giant."

21. Gary Thomas, "Cultivating a Good Marriage," YouTube, https://www.youtube.com/watch?v=zh8GlOcZ0I4.

22. Thomas, *Sacred Marriage*, 213.

23. Ibid., 14.

24. Gary Thomas, "Working Through the Low Points in Marriage," YouTube, February 11, 2010, https://www.youtube .com/watch?v=aDbDBRXYYQA.

25. Gary Thomas, "Staying Committed in Your Marriage," YouTube, Feb. 12, 2010, https://www.youtube.com/ watch?v=x32Bm1D_6MI.

CHAPTER 4
PRUNING THAT LEADS TO INTIMACY

1. Michael L. Parker, *Training and Pruning Fruit Trees*, North Caroline Cooperative Extension Service, http://www.ces.ncsu .edu/depts/hort/hil/ag29.html.

2. Allen Hood, "Responding Well During a Season of Pruning," International House of Prayer, http://www.ihopkc.org/ resources/asset/g77d0srs/auto/true/.

3. Ibid., 4.

4. James and Betty Robison, *Living in Love* (Colorado Springs, Colorado: WaterBrooks Press, 2010), 115–116.

5. Barry and Lori Byrne, *Love After Marriage* (Ventura, California: Regal, 2012, Kindle Edition), 36.

6. Gary Chapman, *Now You're Speaking My Language* (Nashville, Tennessee: BHP Publishing Group, 2007), 7.

CHAPTER 5
THE GLORY OF FATHERS

1.   Cheryl Wetzstein, "Dad, mom in homes is essential Americans say" *The Washington Times*, June 16, 2011, http://washingtontimes.com/news/2011/jun/16/dad-mom-in-home-is-esstential-americans-say/.

2.   Ken R. Canfield, *The 7 Secrets of Effective Fathers* (Carol Streams, Illinois: Tyndale House Publishers, 1992), 225.

3.   James Dobson, *Bringing Up Boys* (Carol Stream, Ill: Tyndale House, 2001), 14.

4.   Hanna Rosin, "New Data on the Rise of Women, December 2010," TEDWomen, http://www.ted.com/talks/hanna_rosin_new_data_on_the_rise_of_women.html.

5.   Dobson, *Bringing Up Boys*, 14.

6.   Ibid., 16.

7.   Ibid.

8.   "Gender-Neutral Restrooms Become Law," NBC10.com, May 10, 2013, http://www.nbcphiladelphia.com/news/local/LGBT-Gender-Neutral -Restrooms-206932591.html.

9.   John Piper and Wayne Grudem, *Recovering Biblical Manhood and Womanhood* (Wheaton, Illinois: Crossway Books, a publishing ministry of Good News Publishers, 1991, 2006 Kindle Edition), 721.

10. Ibid., 779.

11. John Piper, *Seeing and Savoring Jesus Christ* (Wheaton, Illinois: Crossway Books, 2004), 163.

12. Ken Canfield, *The Heart of a Father: How You Can Become a Dad of Destiny* (Chicago, Ill: Northfield Publishing, 1996), 1363.

13. Alex Kendrick and Randy Alcorn, *The Resolution for Men* (Nashville, TN: Kendrick Bros), 19.

14. Kostenberger, *God, Marriage, and Family*, 85–86.

15. Meg Meeker, *Strong Fathers, Strong Daughters: 10 Secrets Every Father Should Know* (Washington, DC: Regnery Publishing, 2006), 8.

16. "Too much time online," iKeepSafe, http://www.ikeepsafe .org/be-a-pro/balance/too-much-time-online/.

17. Severance, "Jonathan Edwards: America's Humble Giant."

18. *The Works of President Edwards in Eight Volumes* (Published at Worcester by Isaiah Thomas, 1808), 834.

CHAPTER 6
EMBRACING MOTHERHOOD

* Elliot, *Let Me Be A Woman*, 58.

1. Ibid., 53.

2. This is defined from www.thefreedictionary.com.

3. "John Wesley Quotes," Preach-the-Gospel.com, http://www .preach-the-gospel.com/John-Wesley-Quotes.htm.

4. Elliot, *Let Me Be A Woman*, 58.

5. June Fuentes, *True Christian Motherhood* (Self-published, Kindle Edition, September 8, 2011), 54–59.

6. Ibid., 70–71.

CHAPTER 7
AIMING YOUR ARROWS

1. Baucham, *Family Driven Faith*, 176.

2. Ibid., 20.

3. Research from Barna Group, barna.org.

CHAPTER 8
DATING GOD'S WAY

* Harris, Joshua, *I Kissed Dating Goodbye* (New York City, NY: The Doubleday, Religious Publishing Group, Kindle Edition, 2012), 29.

1. Ibid., 191.
2. Ibid.
3. Quoted in Harris, *I Kissed Dating Goodbye*, 32.
4. This definition is taken from http://www.merriam-webster.com/dictionary/single.

CHAPTER 9
A PROPHETIC HOME

1. Mike Bickle, "Contending for the Fullness of God's Power," International House of Prayer, August 11, 2006, http://mikebickle.org.
2. Steve Thompson, *You May All Prophesy* (Fort Mills, SC: The Apple Orchard Publishing, 2000), 367
3. Ibid., 90.
4. Mike Bickle, "Receiving Words of Knowledge." International House of Prayer, October 24, 2010, http://mikebickle.org.
5. Wes Hall, Stephen Beauchamp, Ed Hackett, *Cultivating the Gifts* (International House of Prayer, Spring 2009), 62.
6. Mike Bickle, "Pursuing Spiritual Gifts," International House of Prayer, February 9, 2007, http://mikebickle.org.
7. R.A. Torrey, *The Baptism with the Holy Spirit* (Kindle Edition, 2011), 29.
8. John Bevere, *The Holy Spirit: An Introduction* (Palmer Lake, CO: Messenger International, 2013), 2011.

CHAPTER 10
A THOUSAND GENERATIONS

* Don Nori, *Breaking Generational Curses* (Shippensburg, PA: Destiny Image Publishers, 2005), 270.

1. This definition of *legacy* was taken from http://www .merriam-webster.com/dictionary/legacy.

2. J. Otis Ledbetter and Kurt Bruner, "Family Legacies," Focus on the Family, http://www.focusonthefamily.com/parenting/ building_relationships/family_legacies.aspx.

3. Marilyn Hickey, *Breaking Generational Curses* (Tulsa, Oklahoma: Harrison House, 2000), 20.

4. Marilyn Hickey and Sarah Bowling, *Blessing the Next Generation* (New York, NY: Faith Words, eBook, 2008), 397.

5. A.E. Winship, *Jukes-Edwards: A Study in Education and Heredity*, Project Gutenberg, eBook, http://www.gutenberg. org/files/15623/15623-h/15623-h.htm#CHAPTER_III.

6. Ibid.

7. Derek Prince, "Release From the Curse Study: Introduction," Derek Prince Ministries, http://www.derekprince.org/ Articles/1000085366/DPM_US/Archive_of_UK/Keys/ Blessings_and_Curses/Introduction.aspx.

8. Hickey, *Breaking Generational Curses*, 40.

9. Derek Prince, "Release From the Curse Study: Introduction."

10. Nori, *Breaking Generational Curses*, 727.

11. "Life Cycle of a Country," Law Notes, www.1215.org/ lawnotes/work-in-progress/country-life-cycle.htm.

ABOUT ANTONIO AND CHRISTELLE BALDOVINOS

Marked by boldness and passion, Antonio and Christelle Baldovinos have an uncompromising message of calling the church to a wholehearted pursuit after God. They have been involved with missions around the world for more than 17 years. Recently, they have built a growing house of prayer in Alberta, Canada, with corresponding training. Along with being authors and speakers, they have been married since 1997 and have a successful family with five children: Michael, Gabriel, Elijah, Isabella, and Justice.

Contact:

Website: www.antoniobaldovinos.org

Email: info@antoniobaldovinos.org

Twitter: @Antoniobaldov

More about Antonio and Christelle's Ministry

Global Prayer House: www.globalprayerhouse.com

Pursuit Conferences: www.pursuitmovement.com

Pursuit Internship: www.pursuitinternship.com